World Book of **Places to Visit**

MW01658186

World Book of **Places to Visit**

by The Editors of
The World Book Encyclopedia

Published by

World Book, Inc.
a Scott Fetzer company

Chicago

Copyright © 1985, 1981 by
World Book, Inc.
Merchandise Mart Plaza, Chicago, Illinois 60654
All rights reserved. This volume may not be reproduced in whole or in part in any form without written permission from the publishers.
Printed in the United States of America
ISBN 0-7166-3178-4
Library of Congress Catalog Card No. 84-52717
d/he

Contents

Introduction

The *World Book of Places to Visit* is a guide to over 500 interesting, informative, and enjoyable places to visit in the United States and Canada. This convenient handbook not only lists the attractions but tells you where they are and what they are. Descriptions include each site's geographic features, historical significance, available amusements—whatever makes the site a favorite North American attraction.

There are two types of entries in *Places to Visit*. One type, appearing in the section beginning on page 9, gives information about specific places: historic forts, amusement parks, and famous libraries and museums, for example. The second type of entry, beginning on page 109, is devoted to national park systems of the United States and Canada.

The entries at the beginning of the book appear in alphabetical order under five major divisions. The first four organize the United States into major geographical areas: the Northeast, the Midwest, the South, and the West. The last division is for Canadian attractions. All entries provide much information in a small space.

First, the location of an attraction appears. Then follows a brief description of the tourist site, as well as information about the weather in the general area of the site. Approximate low/high temperatures for January and July are indicated in both Fahrenheit and Celsius. Specific information about the time of year each site is open to the public is included in each entry. If an admission fee is required, this information follows next.

Symbols in the entries indicate more important information for visitors to each attraction. A dollar sign ($) indicates that expenses involved in visiting the site may be high. A tepee (▲) means that camping is available at or near the attraction. A square (□) says that hotels and/or motels are conveniently located. And a square with an *R* inside (R) shows that reservations are advisable at these hotels/motels.

Finally, transportation symbols are a guide to how visitors can reach the site. The symbols and their meanings are:

automobile
bus
plane
train, monorail
boat, ferry

The section devoted to U.S. and Canadian national park systems includes, in addition to entries for parks, information about national historic sites of the United States and Canada. Symbols in entries show whether camping or other overnight lodging is available and when the areas are open.

An index of tourist sites by state, province, or territory is included at the back of this guide. And, finally, the guide also contains a listing of tourist information services to contact for each state and Canada.

The Editors

Northeast

Atlantic City, New Jersey

The state's most famous seaside resort. Has a 7-mile (11-kilometer) boardwalk and a convention hall that can seat 41,000 persons. Other seaside resorts along the southeastern coast include Asbury Park, Cape May, North Wildwood, Ocean City, Seaside Heights, Wildwood, and Wildwood Crest.

Jan.: 20/46F (–7/8C); July: 62/84F (17/29C)

Open year-round

$ [R]

Barnegat Lighthouse

Near Barnegat Light, New Jersey

Favorite subject of painters and photographers. Part of a state park that includes a museum and sandy beach.

Jan.: 20/42F (–7/6C); July: 62/84F (17/29C)

Open year-round; admission fee

[R]

Batsto

Near Hammonton, New Jersey

Restored 18th-century iron-making village. Cannon balls and kettles were made here for Washington's army during the Revolutionary War.

Jan.: 20/46F (–7/8C); July: 62/88F (17/31C)

Open year-round

Bennington Battle Monument
Bennington, Vermont
Honors colonists who in 1777 defeated the British in the Battle of Bennington.
Jan.: 10/36F (–12/2C); July: 54/86F (12/30C)
Open March through November; admission fee

Black Mansion
Ellsworth, Maine
Often called Maine's Mount Vernon. Has low porch with five tall columns. Features fine china, silverware, furniture, and winding staircase.
Jan.: 6/34F (–14/1C); July: 54/84F (12/29C)
Open June 1 to October 15; admission fee

Branford Trolley Museum
East Haven, Connecticut
100 trolleys from 1878 to 1936. Museum exhibits, trolley rides, picnic areas.
Jan.: 20/38F (–7/3C); July: 60/84F (16/29C)
Open April through October, weekends—mid-June through mid-September, daily; admission fee

Bunker Hill
In the Charlestown section of Boston, Massachusetts
The 220-foot (67-meter) granite shaft was built between 1825 and 1842. Museum pays tribute to the soldiers who fought in the Battle of Bunker Hill.
Jan.: 20/40F (–7/4C); July: 60/84F (16/29C)
Open year-round

Burnham Tavern
Machias, Maine
Where colonists met in 1775 to plot the capture of the British ship *Margaretta*. The capture was made during the first naval battle of the Revolutionary War. Burnham Tavern, built about 1770, still displays its original sign: "Drink for the thirsty, food for the hungry, lodging for the weary, and good keeping for horses."
Jan.: 12/34F (–11/1C); July: 50/76F (10/24C)
Open mid-June to Labor Day; admission fee

Cape Cod, Massachusetts
A peninsula that is a famous summer resort and vacation area. Faces Cape Cod Bay on the north, Nantucket Sound on the south, and the Atlantic Ocean on the east. Long, sandy beaches stretch along the cape.
Jan.: 24/40F (–4/4C); July: 60/80F (16/27C)
Open year-round

Cliff Walk
Newport, Rhode Island
A 3-mile (5-kilometer) path through scenes of contrasting beauty. On one side of the walk is the rocky Atlantic coast. On the other side are many mansions. The most famous is The Breakers, a 70-room house built for Cornelius Vanderbilt in 1895. Nearby mansion called Marble House is one of the United States' most ornate buildings, built for William K. Vanderbilt in 1892.
Jan.: 20/40F (–7/4C); July: 60/82F (16/28C)
Open year-round

Constitution (Old Ironsides)

Charles River near the Charlestown section of Boston, Massachusetts

This early U.S. Navy frigate became famous during the War of 1812. Oliver Wendell Holmes honored the ship with his famous poem "Old Ironsides."

Jan.: 20/40F (−7/4C); July: 60/84F (16/29C)

Open year-round

[R]

🚗 🚌 ✈

Coolidge Birthplace

Near Plymouth, Vermont

Combination store and post office. Nearby museum houses possessions of President Calvin Coolidge.

Jan.: 6/32F (−14/0C); July: 50/82F (10/28C)

Open mid-May through mid-October; admission fee

▲ [R]

🚗

Corning Glass Center and Steuben Glass Factory

Corning, New York

Includes the world's largest library devoted to glass. Museum with exhibits of 3,500 years of glassmaking.

Jan.: 12/40F (−11/4C); July: 54/86F (12/30C)

Open year-round except Thanksgiving, Christmas Eve, Christmas Day, and New Year's Day; admission fee

▲ [R]

🚗 🚌 ✈

Daniel Webster's Birthplace

Between Salisbury and Franklin, New Hampshire

Two-room cabin houses mementos of the orator.

Jan.: 10/34F (−12/1C); July; 56/84F (13/29C)

Open mid-June through Labor Day, Wednesday through Sunday; admission fee

▲ [R]

🚗

Edison National Historic Site
West Orange, New Jersey
Edison's laboratory and library. Museum features his invention equipment.
Jan.: 20/42F (–7/6C); July: 62/88F (17/31C)
Open year-round except Thanksgiving, Christmas, New Year's Day; admission fee
R

Ephrata Cloisters
Ephrata, Pennsylvania
Restored community built by German Seventh-Day Baptists in 1732. During summer famous Ephrata choir sings and historical pageant takes place.
Jan.: 24/44F (–4/7C); July: 62/92F (17/33C)
Open year-round except holidays; admission fee
R

Farmers' Museum and Village Crossroads
Near Cooperstown, New York
Museum has early agricultural tools and appliances. Nearby Crossroads includes many buildings built in the late 1700's and early 1800's.
Jan.: 12/36F (–11/2C); July: 54/86F (12/30C)
Open year-round; admission fee
R

First Parish Church
Portland, Maine
A Unitarian Church. In 1819 the site of Maine's only constitutional convention.
Jan.: 12/34F (–11/1C); July: 54/80F (12/27C)
Open June through August
R

Fishermen's Memorial
Gloucester, Massachusetts
A statue overlooking the city's harbor. Honors the many members of Gloucester fishing crews who lost their lives. Gloucester has been an important fishing port since colonial days.
Jan.: 20/40F (–7/4C); July: 60/84F (16/29C)
Open year-round

Flagship *Niagara*
Erie, Pennsylvania
Restored ship of Oliver Hazard Perry, who defeated the British navy on Great Lakes during War of 1812.
Jan.: 20/36F (–7/2C); July: 58/84F (14/29C)
Open year-round; admission fee

Flume
Near Lincoln, New Hampshire
A chasm 800 feet (240 meters) long. Visitors can view scenic wilderness on tour through the Flume.
Jan.: 6/30F (–14/–1C); July: 52/80F (11/27C)
Open mid-May through mid-October; admission fee

Fort Ticonderoga
On Lake Champlain, New York
Reconstruction of the colonial fort where Ethan Allen and his Green Mountain Boys defied the British and forced them to surrender in 1775.
Jan.: 6/32F (–14/0C); July: 58/86F (14/30C)
Open mid-May through mid-October; admission fee

Fort Western
Augusta, Maine
Dates from 1754. Where Benedict Arnold and his soldiers met before attacking Quebec in 1775.
Jan.: 6/34F (–14/1C); July: 58/84F (14/29C)
Open 3rd week in May through Labor Day; admission fee
R

Franklin Pierce Homestead
Hillsboro, New Hampshire
Large, two-story house where President Pierce spent his early years. Built in 1804.
Jan.: 6/34F (–14/1C); July: 52/84F (11/29C)
Open June through September; donations
R

Granite Quarries
Millstone Hill in Barre, Vermont
Cut deeply into Millstone Hill. World's largest stone-finishing plant. Granite blocks are quarried and granite is sawed, polished, and carved.
Jan.: 2/28F (–17/–2C); July: 54/82F (12/28C)
Open May through October; free admission, tour fee
R

Groton Monument
Groton, Connecticut
A granite tower 134 feet (41 meters) high. Commemorates the Battle of Fort Griswold in 1782. British troops, led by the traitor Benedict Arnold, massacred patriots they captured in the battle.
Jan.: 20/42F (–7/6C); July: 60/84F (16/29C)
Open year-round; museum, Memorial Day–Labor Day, daily
R

Harvard University
Cambridge, Massachusetts
One of the world's famous universities, founded in 1636. The oldest institute of higher learning in the United States. Harvard Yard, center of the original college, retains much of its early charm.
Jan.: 20/40F (–7/4C); July: 60/84F (16/29C)
Open year-round
[R]

Hawk Mountain Bird Sanctuary
Kittatinny Mountains, between Pennsylvania and northwestern New Jersey
One of the world's few refuges for birds of prey such as eagles and hawks.
Jan.: 16/40F (–9/4C); July: 58/88F (14/31C)
Open year-round except holidays; admission fee
[R]

Howe Caverns
Near Cobleskill, New York
Colorfully lighted caves, some 200 feet (61 meters) underground.
Jan.: 12/36F (–11/2C); July: 58/86F (14/30C)
Open year-round; admission fee
[R]

Hunter House
Newport, Rhode Island
One of America's finest examples of colonial residential architecture. Dates from 1748.
Jan.: 20/40F (–7/4C); July: 60/82F (16/28C)
Open year-round; admission fee
[R]

John and Priscilla Alden House

Duxbury, Massachusetts

Probably the only house still standing that was occupied by Pilgrims who sailed on the *Mayflower*. Built about 1653.

Jan.: 20/40F (–7/4C); July: 60/84F (16/29C)

Open year-round; admission fee

▲ [R]

Kancamagus Highway

Between Lincoln and Conway, New Hampshire

A 34½-mile (55.5-kilometer) road that offers spectacular views of mountains, forests, and streams.

Jan.: 2/34F (–17/1C); July: 52/84F (11/29C)

Open year-round

▲ [R]

Lake Placid

Adirondack Mountains, New York

World-famous resort town. Noted for its glacial lake and excellent facilities for winter and summer sports.

Jan.: 0/28F (–18/–2C); July: 50/78F (10/26C)

Open year-round

▲ □

Marble Quarries and Marble Exhibit

Proctor, Vermont

Quarries among world's largest. Exhibit, in the display rooms of the Vermont Marble Company, features the world's largest collection of various kinds of marble.

Jan.: 10/32F (–12/0C); July: 58/86F (14/30C)

Open mid-May through October; admission fee

▲ [R]

Mark Twain Mansion
Hartford, Connecticut
Home of the famous American author during the late 1800's. The residence has many original furnishings and other personal belongings of the Twain family.
Jan.: 16/38F (−9/3C); July: 60/84F (16/29C)
Open year-round; admission fee

Mount Washington Cog Railway
Near Fabyan, New Hampshire
Runs to the top of Mount Washington. Railway rises 3,625 feet (1,105 meters). Completed in 1869, the first cog railway in North America.
Jan.: 2/30F (−17/−1C); July: 52/80F (11/27C)
Open Memorial Day through Columbus Day; admission fee

Mystic Seaport Museum
Mystic, Connecticut
Recalls Connecticut's seafaring tradition. The seaport has been rebuilt to look like a whaling village of the 1800's.
Jan.: 16/38F (−9/3C); July: 60/84F (16/29C)
Open year-round; admission fee

National Baseball Hall of Fame and Museum
Cooperstown, New York
Honors great baseball players and displays historic equipment of the game.
Jan.: 12/36F (−11/2C); July: 54/86F (12/30C)
Open year-round; admission fee

Niagara Falls
Niagara Falls, New York
Most famous waterfall in the world. About 200,000 short tons (180,000 metric tons) of water plunge into a steep-walled gorge every minute.
Jan.: 18/36F (–8/2C); July: 58/86F (14/30C)
Open year-round
▲ □

Old Constitution House
Windsor, Vermont
Where Vermont's first constitution was written. The two-story frame house, originally a tavern, was built in 1772.
Jan.: 6/32F (–14/0C); July: 54/86F (12/30C)
Open mid-May through mid-October
▲ [R]

Old Fort Niagara
Near Youngstown, New York
Scene of fighting during the French and Indian War and the War of 1812.
Jan.: 18/36F (–8/2C); July: 58/86F (14/30C)
Open year-round except Thanksgiving, Christmas, and New Year's Day; admission fee
▲ [R]

Old Gaol Museum
York, Maine
Oldest public building in Maine. Built in 1653, it served as a gaol, or jail, until 1860.
Jan.: 12/34F (–11/1C); July: 54/84F (12/29C)
Open mid-June to September 30; admission fee
▲ [R]

Old Narragansett Church
North Kingstown, Rhode Island
Oldest Episcopal church in the northern United States. Dates from 1707.
Jan.: 20/40F (–7/4C); July: 60/82F (16/28C)
Open summer by appointment

Old Stone Mill
Newport, Rhode Island
Roofless stone tower. No record of its construction exists, and archaeologists have failed to determine its origin. Local historians believe Vikings built the tower about A.D. 1000.
Jan.: 20/40F (–7/4C); July: 60/82F (16/28C)
Open year-round

Old Sturbridge Village
Sturbridge, Massachusetts
A replica of a typical New England town of the early 1800's.
Jan.: 12/36F (–11/2C); July: 56/84F (13/29C)
Open May through September, daily—October through April, Tuesday through Sunday; admission fee

Pennsylvania Farm Museum of Landis Valley
Near Lancaster, Pennsylvania
Tells story of Pennsylvania's village and farm life from the 1800's until modern times.
Jan.: 28/44F (–4/7C); July: 62/92F (17/33C)
Open year-round; admission fee

Penobscot Marine Museum

Searsport, Maine

Displays valuable paintings, ship models, old sailing charts, navigation instruments, fishing and whaling equipment, ships' logs, and other historical items.

Jan.: 12/34F (–11/1C); July: 54/84F (12/29C)

Open May 24 to October 15; admission fee

Pine Creek Gorge

Near Wellsboro, Pennsylvania

Beautiful canyon, 1,100 feet (335 meters) deep, dug thousands of years ago by the Pine Creek River. Known as the Grand Canyon of Pennsylvania.

Jan.: 16/36F (–9/2C); July: 54/84F (12/29C)

Open year-round

Plimoth Plantation

Plymouth, Massachusetts

A reconstruction of the first Pilgrim village. Maintains *Mayflower II*, built the way the original *Mayflower* is thought to have looked.

Jan.: 20/40F (–7/4C); July: 60/84F (16/29C)

Open April through November; admission fee

Portland Head Light

Near Portland, Maine

Towers 101 feet (31 meters) over the surf. Built in 1791. One of the most famous American lighthouses.

Jan.: 12/34F (–11/1C); July: 54/80F (12/27C)

Open year-round

Princeton, New Jersey
Home of Princeton University and Princeton Battlefield. University's Nassau Hall served as the U.S. Capitol in 1783.
Jan.: 24/42F (–4/6C); July: 62/88F (17/31C)
Open year-round
[R]

Profile Mountain (Cannon Mountain)
Near Easton, New Hampshire
Features a rock formation that looks like the side view of an old man's face. The formation, called the Old Man of the Mountain, was made famous by Nathaniel Hawthorne's short story "The Great Stone Face."
Jan.: 6/30F (–14/–1C); July: 52/80F (11/27C)
Open year-round
▲ [R]

Roadside America
Near Hamburg, Pennsylvania
Indoor miniature village telling story of American life from pioneer days to present.
Jan.: 20/40F (–7/4C); July: 58/88F (14/31C)
Open year-round; admission fee
▲ □

Rockville Bridge
Near Harrisburg, Pennsylvania
Stretches 3,820 feet (1,164 meters) across the Susquehanna River. One of the world's largest arch stone bridges.
Jan.: 20/44F (–7/7C); July: 62/88F (17/31C)
Open year-round
▲ □

Saranac Lake
Adirondacks, New York
Famous summer and winter sports center.
Jan.: 0/28F (–18/–2C); July: 50/78F (10/26C)
Open year-round

Saratoga Springs, New York
Noted for its race tracks and for its health resort owned and operated by the state. National Museum of Racing has many exhibits of famous Thoroughbred horses.
Jan.: 12/32F (–11/0C); July: 58/86F (14/30C)
Open year-round; admission fee
[R]

Seashore Trolley Museum
Near Kennebunkport, Maine
Largest U.S. museum that exhibits only electric railroad equipment.
Jan.: 12/34F (–11/1C); July: 54/84F (12/29C)
Open Memorial Day to mid-June and mid-September to October, weekends—mid-June to mid-September, daily; admission fee
[R]

Shelburne Museum
Shelburne, Vermont
Reconstruction of an early American village. Includes more than 30 historic buildings. Side-wheeler steamship *Ticonderoga* is a part of the museum.
Jan.: 6/32F (–14/0C); July: 58/86F (14/30C)
Open mid-May through mid-October; admission fee

Six Flags Great Adventure
Jackson, New Jersey
Combination 450-acre (180-hectare) safari park and amusement park. About 2,000 exotic animals are free to roam the grounds of the safari park. The amusement park has many rides, live shows, and circus acts.
Jan.: 20/42F (–7/6C); July: 62/88F (17/31C)
Open April through mid-October; admission fee
▲ [R]
🚗 🚌

Slater Mill Historic Site
Pawtucket, Rhode Island
Contains one of the first successful textile mills in North America. Mill built in 1793 by Samuel Slater, founder of the American textile industry. Now a museum, the mill has been called the Cradle of American Industry.
Jan.: 16/40F (–9/4C); July: 62/88F (17/31C)
Open March through December; admission fee
[R]
🚗 🚌

Smuggler's Notch
Near Stowe, Vermont
Wide gap between Mount Mansfield and Sterling Mountains. Name originated during the War of 1812, when smugglers brought goods through the notch from Canada to Boston.
Jan.: 2/28F (–17/–2C); July: 54/82F (12/28C)
Open April through December
▲ □
🚗

Strasburg Rail Road
Strasburg (Lancaster County), Pennsylvania
Still operates on old-time steam equipment. One of the United States' oldest chartered, short-line railroads.
Jan.: 28/44F (−4/7C); July 62/92F (17/33C)
Open March through December; admission fee
▲ [R]

Strawbery Banke
Portsmouth, New Hampshire
Restored colonial seaport. Features homes built in the 1700's and 1800's, craft shops, and historical exhibits.
Jan.: 14/38F (−10/3C); July: 56/84F (13/29C)
Open April 15 through November 15; admission fee
▲ [R]

Touro Synagogue
Newport, Rhode Island
Oldest existing U.S. synagogue. Dates from 1763.
Jan.: 20/40F (−7/4C); July: 60/82F (16/28C)
Open year-round
[R]

United States Military Academy
West Point, New York
Located on the Hudson River north of New York City. The oldest military college in the United States.
Jan.: 18/40F (−8/4C); July: 62/86F (17/30C)
Open year-round
▲ [R]

Valley Railroad
Essex, Connecticut
Old-fashioned train with steam locomotive and restored vintage coaches. Runs from century-old Essex depot to Connecticut River and connects with a river boat cruise.
Jan.: 16/38F (−9/3C); July: 60/84F (16/29C)
Open May through October, daily; admission fee
R

Vernon Valley/Action Park
Great Gorge, New Jersey
New Jersey's largest ski area.
Jan.: 24/46F (−4/8C); July: 62/88F (17/31C)
Open year-round; admission fee
R

Wadsworth-Longfellow House
Portland, Maine
Boyhood home of Henry Wadsworth Longfellow.
Jan.: 12/34F (−11/1C); July: 54/80F (12/27C)
Open June 1 to September 30; admission fee
R

Walden Pond
Near Concord, Massachusetts
Small lake near which Henry David Thoreau lived for two years. Thoreau described his experiences at the pond in *Walden*.
Jan.: 20/40F (−7/4C); July: 60/84F (16/29C)
Open year-round; admission fee
R

Waterloo Village
Byram/Stanhope, New Jersey
Restored 18th-century historic village on Morris Canal. Features museums, shops, and concerts.
Jan.: 20/42F (−7/6C); July: 58/84F (14/29C)
Open April through December; admission fee
[R]

Wheaton Village
Millville, New Jersey
Recreated 1888 glassmaking town. Features museums, glassmaking demonstrations, crafts, and Victorian-era buildings.
Jan.: 24/46F (−4/8C); July: 62/88F (17/31C)
Open year-round except Thanksgiving, Christmas, New Year's Day, Easter Sunday; admission fee
[R]

White Horse Tavern
Newport, Rhode Island
An active tavern, the oldest original tavern building in America. Licensed in 1683, built in 1673.
Jan.: 20/40F (−7/4C); July: 60/82F (16/28C)
Open year-round
[R]

Witch House
Salem, Massachusetts
The home of Jonathan Corwin, a judge at the Salem witchcraft trials in the 1690's.
Jan.: 20/40F (−7/4C); July: 60/84F (16/29C)
Open March through November, daily; admission fee
[R]

Midwest

Amana Colonies
Southwest of Cedar Rapids, Iowa
Seven villages having interesting museums and popular restaurants. Visitors may watch craftsworkers build furniture, make yarn, and weave fabrics.
Jan.: 8/30F (−13/−1C); July: 58/86F (14/30C)
Open year-round

Arbor Lodge
Nebraska City, Nebraska
Home of Julius Sterling Morton, a Nebraska journalist and the founder of Arbor Day. The 52-room mansion, built as a 4-room house in 1855 and enlarged several times, has elegant furnishings.
Jan.: 10/36F (−12/2C); July: 66/92F (19/33C)
Open mid-April to early November; admission fee

Automobile Plants
Dearborn, Detroit, Flint, Lansing, and Pontiac, Michigan (the immediate Detroit area)
Guided tours for visitors. Big Three automotive companies, Chrysler, Ford, and GM.
Jan.: 16/36F (−9/2C); July: 60/90F (16/32C)
Open year-round

Bellevue, Nebraska

Oldest town in Nebraska. Established about 1823 as a fur-trading center. Some buildings more than 100 years old.

Jan.: 10/36F (–12/2C); July: 66/92F (19/33C)

Open year-round

[R]

Beverly Shores, Indiana

Residential village on Lake Michigan. Has many houses from the 1933–1934 Century of Progress Exposition in Chicago.

Jan.: 14/36F (–10/2C); July: 62/86F (17/30C)

Open year-round

▲ □

Big Spring (*Kitchi-ti-ki-pi*)

Near Manistique, Michigan

Pool fed by more than 200 bubbling springs. It is 45 feet (14 meters) deep. Water is so clear that visitors can watch coins drift to the bottom of pool.

Jan.: 8/36F (–13/2C); July: 52/78F (11/26C)

Open year-round; admission fee

□

Bishop Hill

Near Galva, Illinois

Site of a religious community founded in 1846 by Swedish settlers led by Eric Janson. Several of the old buildings still stand. Also has a collection of American primitive paintings.

Jan.: 14/36F (–10/2C); July: 62/92F (17/33C)

Open April through November; museums open year-round

▲ [R]

Blue Hole

Near Castalia, Ohio

Flowing spring that pours forth 10 million gallons (38 million liters) of water daily. Has a constant temperature of 48F (9C).

Jan.: 22/38F (–6/3C); July: 62/88F (17/31C)

Open late April to late May, weekends—Memorial Day to Labor Day, daily; admission fee

Boys Town

Near Omaha, Nebraska

Home for neglected and homeless boys of all races and creeds.

Jan.: 10/36F (–12/2C); July: 66/92F (19/33C)

Open year-round

Brookfield Zoo

Near Chicago, Illinois

Officially the Chicago Zoological Park, this is one of the nation's finest zoos. Moats used rather than bars to separate the animals from the visitors.

Jan.: 14/36F (–10/2C); July: 62/84F (17/29C)

Open year-round; admission fee

R

Brown County Art Galleries

Nashville, Indiana

Have exhibits of doll- and pottery-making, metalcraft, weaving, and woodworking.

Jan.: 22/44F (–6/7C); July: 62/90F (17/32C)

Open mid-February to mid-December; admission fee

R

Brownville, Nebraska
A leading river port of the 1850's. Many colorful reminders of pioneer days still stand.
Jan.: 14/40F (–10/4C); July: 66/92F (19/33C)
Open May to October; admission fee
▲ [R]

Burning Lignite Beds
Near Amidon, North Dakota
Can be seen from a great distance at night. Lignite beds were probably set afire by lightning or by prairie fires or campfires. Fire has advanced slowly, although it has been burning for many years.
Jan.: 0/30F (–18/–1C); July: 54/86F (12/30C)
Open during summer months
▲ [R]

Campus Martius State Memorial Museum
Marietta, Ohio
Stands on the site of the fortified stockade built by the first permanent white settlers in Ohio. Nearby Ohio River Museum exhibits models, pictures, and relics of riverboats.
Jan.: 22/46F (–6/8C); July: 62/92F (17/33C)
Open March through November; admission fee
[R]

Cave of the Mounds
Between Mount Horeb and Blue Mounds, Wisconsin
Limestone cavern decorated with hundreds of colorful crystal formations hanging from ceiling, rising from floor.
Jan.: 8/30F (–13/1C); July: 58/86F (15/30C)
Open year-round; admission fee
▲ [R]

Chalk Beds
Gove and Trego counties, Kansas
Contain the fossil remains of many prehistoric animals.
Jan.: 12/48F (–11/9C); July: 60/96F (16/36C)
Open year-round

Chateau De Mores
Near Medora, North Dakota
Home of a Frenchman, the Marquis de Mores, who founded Medora in 1883.
Jan.: 0/30F (–18/1C); July: 54/86F (12/30C)
Open April 15 to October 15; admission fee

Circus World Museum
Baraboo, Wisconsin
Has large collection of equipment used by U.S. circuses. Displays include items used by the Ringling brothers, who started their world-famous circus in Baraboo in 1884. Small circus show is held in summer.
Jan.: 8/30F (–13/1C); July: 62/86F (17/30C)
Open mid-May through mid-September; admission fee

Climatron
Missouri Botanical Garden, St. Louis, Missouri
A revolutionary greenhouse. The great domed structure is completely air-conditioned and moisture controlled. Displays a variety of plants.
Jan.: 20/46F (–7/8C); July: 64/92F (18/33C)
Open year-round; admission fee

Conner Prairie Pioneer Settlement
Noblesville, Indiana
Has exhibits illustrating life in Indiana during the early 1800's.
Jan.: 18/40F (– 8/4C); July: 62/90F (17/32C)
Open first Wednesday in April through second Sunday in November; admission fee

Corn Palace
Mitchell, South Dakota
Redecorated every fall with murals made of different colors of corn and other grains. Many events held.
Jan.: 4/34F (– 16/1C); July: 58/92F (14/33C)
Open June to September

Crazy Horse Memorial
Near Custer, South Dakota
Gigantic sculpture of Sioux chief being carved in a granite mountain by Korczak Ziolkowski.
Jan.: 0/40F (– 18/4C); July: 46/88 (8/31C)
Open year-round; admission fee

Deadwood
In the Black Hills, South Dakota
Brawling mining town of the Old West, has many reminders of its wild early days. Wild Bill Hickok and other famous people buried in Boot Hill Cemetery.
Jan.: 8/40F (– 13/4C); July: 46/88F (8/31C)
Attractions open from mid-May to mid-October; some admission fees

Dickson Mounds

Near Lewistown, Illinois

Lies in a 63-acre (25-hectare) park. An Indian mound has been partly dug open to show skeletons, tools, and weapons in the positions in which they were buried 500 to 1,000 years ago. Museum has relics of the Stone Age and early Indian life.

Jan.: 18/40F (−8/4C); July: 62/92F (17/33C)

Open year-round

Dodge House

Council Bluffs, Iowa

Restored home of railroad builder Grenville M. Dodge. Dodge served as the chief engineer for construction of the Union Pacific Railroad, which became part of the first transcontinental railroad system in the United States.

Jan.: 12/34F (−11/1C); July: 66/90F (19/32C)

Open year-round except in January, on Monday, Christmas, and Thanksgiving; admission fee

Dvořák Memorial

Spillville, Iowa

Honors a visit by the Czech composer Antonín Dvořák in 1893. While in Spillville, he worked on his famous *Symphony in E minor: From the New World*. A collection of clocks carved by the Bily brothers, Czech craftsworkers, is housed in a building where Dvořák lived.

Jan.: 4/30F (−16/−1C); July: 58/86F (14/30C)

Open May through October, daily—March and November, weekends; admission fee

Eisenhower Library and Museum
Abilene, Kansas
House mementos and papers of President Dwight D. Eisenhower. His boyhood home and grave are nearby.
Jan.: 16/44F (–9/7C); July: 64/96F (18/36C)
Open year-round; admission fee

Fort Abercrombie
Abercrombie, North Dakota
First U.S. military post in present-day North Dakota. Established in 1857.
Jan.: –4/24F (–20/–4C); July: 58/86F (14/30C)
Open May 15 to September 15; admission fee

Fort Leavenworth
Near Leavenworth, Kansas
Founded in 1827, the first permanent white settlement in Kansas. The fort now houses the U.S. Army Command and General Staff College, and Leavenworth Prison, a federal penitentiary.
Jan.: 20/44F (–7/7C); July: 68/94F (20/34C)
Open year-round

Fort Michilimackinac
Mackinaw City, Michigan
Reconstruction of the fort built in the 1700's. Buildings include Ste. Anne's Jesuit church and the home of British Commander Robert Rogers.
Jan.: 12/32F (–11/0C); July: 56/78F (13/26C)
Open May through October; admission fee

Fort Recovery State Memorial
Village of Fort Recovery, Ohio
Reproduction of part of the fort built in 1793 by General Anthony Wayne. Fort used during Indian wars.
Jan.: 18/38F (–8/3C); July: 62/88F (17/31C)
Open May through Labor Day; admission fee
▲

Fort Riley
Near Junction City, Kansas
Became famous as a cavalry center. Many interesting buildings, including an early Kansas capitol and General George A. Custer's home, stand on the grounds.
Jan.: 16/44F (–9/7C); July: 64/94F (18/34C)
Open year-round
▲ □

Fort Snelling
Near Minneapolis, Minnesota
A restored military post built in the 1820's. Features demonstrations dealing with military life then.
Jan.: 6/24F (–14/–4C); July: 60/86F (16/30C)
Open June through October; admission fee
[R]

Front Street and Boot Hill
Dodge City, Kansas
The colorful main street of old-time Dodge City. Has been recreated as it looked in the 1870's. A museum and the old cemetery reflect Dodge City's famous cow-town history.
Jan.: 16/48F (–9/9C); July: 64/98F (18/37C)
Open year-round; admission fee
▲ [R]

Gateway Arch
St. Louis, Missouri
Commemorates the city's role in Western settlement. Tallest monument constructed in the United States.
Jan.: 20/46F (−7/8C); July: 64/92F (18/33C)
Open year-round; tour fee
□

Great Lakes of South Dakota
Missouri River, South Dakota
Formed by four huge dams on the Missouri River. The four lakes offer many water sports, including excellent walleye fishing. Visitors may tour power plants of the dams.
Jan.: −4/40F (−20/4C); July: 46/96F (8/36C)
Open year-round
[R]

Great Serpent Mound
Near Hillsboro, Ohio
One of the world's best-known prehistoric structures. The mound, shaped like a snake, has seven deep curves. It rises about 4 feet (1.2 meters) and extends over ¼ mile (0.4 kilometer).
Jan.: 22/42F (−6/6C); July: 60/88F (16/31C)
Open Memorial Day through October
[R]

Greenfield Village
Dearborn, Michigan
Collection of historic buildings restored by Henry Ford. Henry Ford Museum is next to village.
Jan.: 16/36F (−9/2C); July: 60/90F (16/32C)
Open year-round; admission fee
□

Grotto of the Redemption
West Bend, Iowa
A religious structure begun by Father Paul M. Dobberstein in 1912. The walls of this artificial grotto, or cave, portray humanity's fall from divine grace and its redemption.
Jan.: 8/30F (–13/–1C); July: 62/90F (17/32C)
Open year-round

R

Guthrie Theater
Minneapolis, Minnesota
Strikingly designed playhouse that opened in 1963. A company of actors presents plays every year.
Jan.: 6/24F (–14/–4C); July: 60/86F (16/30C)
Open year-round; admission fee

R

Harry S. Truman Library
Independence, Missouri
Houses about 3½ million documents dealing with the history of U.S. foreign relations.
Jan.: 20/42F (–7/6C); July: 68/92F (20/33C)
Open year-round; admission fee

High Falls
On the Pigeon River in Cook County, Minnesota
Plunges over cliffs that are 133 feet (41 meters) high. Nearby are the remains of Fort Charlotte, an important trading post of the late 1700's.
Jan.: 6/28F (–14/–2C); July: 48/74F (9/23C)
Open year-round

R

Hollenberg Station
Hanover, Kansas
The only station on the pony express route that looks as it did in the early 1860's. One of the first stops for westbound pony express riders.
Jan.: 16/40F (−9/4C); July: 64/94F (18/34C)
Open year-round

House on the Rock
North of Dodgeville, Wisconsin
A 13-room home that sits atop a huge chimney rock rising 450 feet (137 meters) above a valley. Has 6 fireplaces, 4 pools, and many antiques.
Jan.: 8/30F (−13/−1C); July: 58/86F (15/30C)
Open April through November; admission fee

International Peace Garden
In North Dakota and Manitoba
Symbolizes the long friendship between the United States and Canada.
Jan.: −8/18F (−22/−8C); July: 54/82F (12/28C)
Open year-round; admission fee

John Brown Memorial State Park
Osawatomie, Kansas
Marks the site of an early battle over slavery. John Brown led Free Staters against a group that favored slavery. Brown's cabin still stands.
Jan.: 20/44F (−7/7C); July: 68/94F (20/34C)
Open year-round

Kelleys Island

Lake Erie near Sandusky, Ohio

Summer resort famous for its glacial markings and Inscription Rock. The markings are among the world's best examples of glacial action. Rock has traces of prehistoric Indian carvings.

Jan.: 22/38F (−6/3C); July: 62/88F (17/31C)

Open year-round

Lake of the Ozarks

Central Missouri

One of the world's largest artificial lakes. Has a shoreline of more than 1,300 miles (2,090 kilometers).

Jan.: 20/46F (−7/8C); July: 64/92F (18/33C)

Open year-round

Lake Sakakawea

North of Bismarck, North Dakota

Reservoir for Garrison Dam. Popular for swimming, boating, fishing, camping, and picnicking.

Jan.: −4/24F (−20/−4C); July: 54/86F (12/30C)

Open year-round; admission fee

Lincoln Boyhood National Memorial

Near Lincoln City, Indiana

Farm where Abraham Lincoln lived from age 7 to 21. His mother, Nancy Hanks Lincoln, is buried there.

Jan.: 26/48F (−3/9C); July: 66/94F (19/34C)

Open year-round except Christmas and New Year's Day

Lincoln Pioneer Village
Rockport, Indiana
Memorial to Lincoln's 14 years in Indiana. Stockade around 17 log buildings with pioneer articles.
Jan.: 26/48F (–3/9C); July: 66/94F (19/34C)
Open year-round; admission fee

Lincoln's New Salem State Historic Site
Petersburg, Illinois
Has a reproduction of the town in which Abraham Lincoln lived from 1831 to 1837. Buildings include the tavern and store of which Lincoln was part owner and the old cooper's shop where Lincoln studied at night.
Jan.: 18/40F (–8/4C); July: 62/92F (17/33C)
Open year-round, except major holidays
R

Little Brown Church
Near Nashua, Iowa
Stands on the site that inspired William S. Pitts to write the hymn "The Little Brown Church in the Vale."
Jan.: 8/30F (–13/–1C); July: 62/86F (17/30C)
Open year-round
R

Little Norway
Near Mount Horeb, Wisconsin
Built in 1926, resembles a tiny Norwegian village of the early 1800's. The 160-acre (65-hectare) tract has picturesque houses with Scandinavian-style furnishings.
Jan.: 8/30F (–13/-1C); July: 58/86F (15/30C)
Open May 1 through late October; admission fee
R

Living History Farms
Near Des Moines, Iowa
Show agricultural life in Iowa about 1840 and 1900. The attraction also has a farm of the future.
Jan.: 12/34F (–11/1C); July: 62/90F (17/32C)
Open April 14 through October 26; admission fee
[R]

Lumbertown, USA
Brainerd, Minnesota
A reconstruction of a typical early logging town.
Jan.: –6/24F (–21/–4C); July: 56/86F (13/30C)
Open June 15 through Labor Day; admission fee
[R]

Mackinac Island
Straits of Mackinac, between the Upper and Lower peninsulas, Michigan
A famous resort island. No automobiles are permitted on the island.
Jan.: 8/32F (–13/0C); July: 52/78F (11/26C)
Open Memorial Day to mid-October; ferry fee, tour fee
$ [R]

Mark Twain Cave
Near Hannibal, Missouri
A cave that the famous author Mark Twain learned about as a boy. In the novel *The Adventures of Tom Sawyer*, Tom and his friend Becky Thatcher become lost in this cave. Mark Twain Home and Museum nearby in Hannibal.
Jan.: 16/42F (–9/6C); July: 64/92F (18/33C)
Open year-round; admission fee

Mayo Clinic and Foundation
Rochester, Minnesota
Offers tours of the world-famous medical center.
Jan.: 6/28F (−14/−2C); July: 56/86F (13/30C)
Open year-round
[R]

Meramec Caverns
Near Sullivan, Missouri
A legendary hideout of the outlaw Jesse James. First room of this huge cave can hold 300 automobiles.
Jan.: 20/46F (−7/8C); July: 64/92F (18/33C)
Open year-round; admission fee
▲ □

National Professional Football Hall of Fame
Canton, Ohio
Honors outstanding professional football players. Includes museum of equipment worn by famous players and used in famous games.
Jan.: 18/38F (−8/3C); July: 60/84F (16/29C)
Open year-round; admission fee
[R]

Nauvoo, Illinois
Founded as a Mormon community by Joseph Smith on the banks of the Mississippi River in 1839. Visitors may see the homes of Smith and of Brigham Young and Wilford Woodruff, two of the early Twelve Apostles of the Mormon Church.
Jan.: 18/40F (−8/4C); July: 66/92F (19/33C)
Open year-round
▲ [R]

Northwest Angle
Northern Minnesota
The northernmost part of the United States outside Alaska. A scenic boat trip runs from Warroad across Lake of the Woods to the angle.
Jan.: –12/16F (–24/–9C); July: 52/80F (11/27C)
Open year-round

Old World Wisconsin
Near Eagle, Wisconsin
Outdoor museum containing houses and other structures Wisconsin immigrants built in 1800's.
Jan.: 12/34F (–11/1C); July: 58/86F (15/30C)
Open May through October; admission fee

Parke County, Indiana
Has more than 30 covered bridges. Structure over Sugar Creek is 207 feet (63 meters) long. The longest single-span covered bridge in the country.
Jan.: 18/40F (–8/4C); July: 62/90F (17/32C)
Open year-round

Pony Express Stables
St. Joseph, Missouri
Preserved to help trace the heritage of the famed pony express. Riders carried U.S. mail between St. Joseph and Sacramento, California, from April 1860 to October 1861.
Jan.: 16/38F (–9/3C); July: 64/92F (18/33C)
Open year-round; admission fee

Rutherford B. Hayes Library and Museum

Fremont, Ohio

At the former President's Spiegel Grove estate. Library has papers of Hayes and books on American life during the 1800's. Museum features exhibits on the life and times of Hayes and his family.

Jan.: 22/38F (–6/3C); July: 62/88F (17/31C)

Open year-round; admission fee

[R]

SAC Museum

Bellevue, Nebraska

Museum of the U.S. Air Force Strategic Air Command. Offutt Air Force Base is the headquarters of the Strategic Air Command.

Jan.: 10/36F (–12/2C); July: 66/92F (19/33C)

Open year-round; admission fee

[R]

Santa Claus, Indiana

Town that remails thousands of letters and parcels with its postmark at Christmastime. Amusement park, deer farm, statue of Santa Claus, and miniature railroad and circus.

Jan.: 26/48F (–3/9C); July: 66/94F (19/34C)

Open year-round

[R]

Scouts Rest Ranch

Near North Platte, Nebraska

Home of Buffalo Bill. Rehearsal site of Wild West Show.

Jan.: 10/40F (–12/4C); July: 58/92F (14/33C)

Open year-round; admission fee

[R]

Sibley House
Mendota, Minnesota
The oldest stone house in Minnesota. Built in 1835, it has displays of pioneer furniture.
Jan.: 6/24F (–14/–4C); July: 60/86F (16/30C)
Open May through October; admission fee
[R]

Silver Dollar City
Near Branson, Missouri
Reconstruction of an early American mining town. Craftworkers show how Conestoga wagons were built and demonstrate crafts such as candle dipping and glass blowing.
Jan.: 24/50F (–4/10C); July: 64/92F (18/33C)
Open April through October; admission fee
▲ □

Soo Locks
At Sault Ste. Marie, Michigan
Huge locks permit ships to travel between Lakes Huron and Superior.
Jan.: 4/28F (–16/–2C); July: 48/78F (9/26C)
Open spring to fall
▲ □

Statues of Paul Bunyan and Babe
Bemidji, Minnesota
Honor the legendary lumberman and his giant blue ox.
Jan.: –6/20F (–21/–7C); July: 52/86F (11/30C)
Open year-round
▲ [R]

Stuhr Museum of the Prairie Pioneer
Near Grand Island, Nebraska
Features a restored railroad town of the 1800's. A bank, general store, and post office are among 56 original buildings moved to the town.
Jan.: 10/40F (–12/4C); July: 62/94F (17/34C)
Open year-round; admission fee

Tahquamenon Falls
Near Newberry, Michigan
Among the beautiful sights of the Upper Peninsula. Henry Wadsworth Longfellow wrote about both the upper and lower falls of the Tahquamenon River in his poem *The Song of Hiawatha.*
Jan.: 8/28F (–13/–2C); July: 52/84F (11/29C)
Open year-round; admission fee

Toadstool Park
In the Badlands, northwest of Crawford, Nebraska
Has huge, oddly shaped rock formations. Many resemble giant toadstools.
Jan.: 10/36F (–12/2C); July: 58/92F (14/33C)
Open year-round

United States Ski Hall of Fame
Ishpeming, Michigan
Honors famous U.S. skiers, skiing events, and persons who have made outstanding contributions to the sport.
Jan.: 8/28F (–13/–2C); July: 56/78F (13/26C)
Open year-round; admission fee

Vandalia State House

Vandalia, Illinois

Attractive colonial building that was the state capitol from 1836 to 1839. Abraham Lincoln served as a state representative in Vandalia.

Jan.: 22/44F (–6/7C); July: 66/92F (19/33C)

Open year-round except Thanksgiving, Christmas, and New Year's Day

▲ [R]

Winston Churchill Memorial and Library

Fulton, Missouri

Formerly the Church of St. Mary Aldermanbury. Dismantled and moved from London after World War II and rebuilt on the campus of Westminster College in Fulton. Winston Churchill delivered his famous "iron curtain" speech on the campus in 1946.

Jan.: 20/46F (–7/8C); July: 64/92F (18/33C)

Open year-round; admission fee

▲ □

Wisconsin Dells

Adams, Columbia, Juneau, and Sauk counties, Wisconsin

One of the state's most beautiful regions. Wisconsin River has cut a channel 7 miles (11 kilometers) long and 100 feet (30 meters) deep through soft sandstone. Weird formations carved from the rock have colorful names such as Devil's Elbow, Grand Piano, and Fat Man's Misery.

Jan.: 4/30F (–16/–1C); July: 54/90F (12/32C)

Open May through September

$ ▲ [R]

Wright-Patterson Air Force Base
Near Dayton, Ohio
Largest U.S. Air Force research field in the United States. Includes national aeronautics museum and field where Wright brothers conducted experiments.
Jan.: 22/42F (–6/6C); July: 62/88F (17/31C)
Open year-round

Writing Rock
Near Grenora, North Dakota
Large glacial boulder covered with Indian picture writing.
Jan.: –8/18F (–22/–8C); July: 54/86F (12/30C)
Open year-round
R

Wyandotte Cave
Near Leavenworth, Indiana
One of the largest caverns in the United States. Has 5 levels, 35 miles (56 kilometers) of underground passageways, and many large chambers.
Jan.: 26/48F (–3/9C); July: 66/94F (19/34C)
Open year-round; admission fee

Zoar Village State Memorial
Near New Philadelphia, Ohio
Founded in 1817 by Germans seeking freedom from religious persecution. Includes home of their leader, Joseph Bimeler. Also includes gardens and old-fashioned stores.
Jan.: 22/42F (–6/6C); July: 60/88F (16/31C)
Open Memorial Day through October; admission fee

South

Alabama Space and Rocket Center
Tranquility Base, Huntsville, Alabama
Houses the world's largest collection of missiles, space equipment, and related exhibits.
Jan.: 30/52F (1/11C); July: 66/92F (19/33C)
Open year-round; admission fee
[R]

Alamance Battleground
Near Burlington, North Carolina
Scene of a historic battle shortly before the American Revolutionary War. About 2,000 frontier dwellers, who were called the Regulators, rebelled against the eastern planters and finally suffered heroic defeat on May 16, 1771.
Jan.: 30/58F (−1/14C); July: 66/92F (19/33C)
Open year-round Tuesday through Saturday
[R]

Alamo
Downtown San Antonio, Texas
The low, gray chapel of an old Spanish mission. The Alamo was the site of a famous battle in 1836 during the Texas Revolution.
Jan.: 38/70F (3/21C); July: 70/98F (21/37C)
Open year-round
[R]

American Museum of Science and Energy
Oak Ridge, Tennessee
Features exhibits on energy, including displays on the peaceful uses of nuclear energy.
Jan.: 28/50F (–2/10C); July: 64/90F (18/32C)
Open year-round
□

Amstel House
New Castle, Delaware
House of the New Castle Historical Society. Built in the early 1700's. Its colonial exhibits include arts, handicrafts, and furnishings.
Jan.: 26/44F (–3/7C); July: 64/86F (18/30C)
Open year-round except holidays; admission fee
□

Antietam National Battlefield
Sharpsburg, Maryland
Scene of the bloodiest single-day battle of the Civil War.
Jan.: 24/44F (–4/7C); July: 62/92F (17/33C)
Open year-round
▲ □

Avery Island
Near New Iberia, Louisiana
Wooded island lies among sea marshes and swampy thickets. It covers a huge salt deposit. Plants from all parts of the world can be seen in the island's Jungle Gardens, which also contain an egret sanctuary.
Jan.: 42/66F (6/19C); July: 72/94F (22/34C)
Open year-round; admission fee
[R]

Battlegrounds
Near Gaffney, South Carolina
Kings Mountain National Military Park and Cowpens National Battlefield mark the sites of major Revolutionary War battles.
Jan.: 30/58F (–1/14C); July: 66/92F (19/33C)
Open year-round except Christmas Day

Battleship U.S.S. *Alabama* Memorial Park
Mobile, Alabama
Visitors may board World War II Battleship *Alabama* and the USS *Drum*, a submarine anchored alongside.
Jan.: 42/64F (6/18C); July: 70/92F (21/33C)
Open year-round; admission fee

Beauvoir
Biloxi, Mississippi
Jefferson Davis' last home. Now a shrine and museum.
Jan.: 44/64F (7/18C); July: 74/90F (23/32C)
Open year-round; admission fee

Bentonville Battleground
Near Smithfield, North Carolina
Scene of one of the last important Civil War battles. In March 1865, General William T. Sherman defeated Confederate General Joseph E. Johnston.
Jan.: 30/58F (–1/14C); July: 66/96F (19/36C)
Open year-round Tuesday through Saturday

Berkeley Springs
Morgan County, West Virginia
Health resort city long called Bath after the famous British resort city. George Washington noticed the health-giving qualities of the springs while surveying.
Jan.: 24/48F (–4/9C); July: 60/92F (16/33C)
Open year-round; admission fee

Biltmore House and Gardens
Near Asheville, North Carolina
Covers about 12,000 acres (4,860 hectares) of forests and farmlands. Biltmore House, a masterpiece of early French Renaissance architecture, is the chief feature.
Jan.: 26/54F (–3/12C); July: 58/88F (14/31C)
Open year-round; admission fee
$

Blanchard Springs Caverns
Near Mountain View, Arkansas
Have many beautiful formations. Picnicking and swimming available nearby.
Jan.: 24/52F (–4/11C); July: 66/94F (19/34C)
Open year-round; admission fee

Blennerhassett Island
In the Ohio River near Parkersburg, West Virginia
Site of mansion of Harman Blennerhassett, who, with Aaron Burr and others, was suspected of planning an independent government in the Southwest.
Jan.: 24/44F (–4/7C); July: 64/92F (18/33C)
Open summer and fall, Sundays; admission fee

Breaks Interstate Park
Near Elkhorn City, Kentucky
Where the Russell Fork plunges about 350 feet (107 meters) over a distance of 5 miles (8 kilometers) to join the Big Sandy River.
Jan.: 28/52F (–2/11C); July: 64/88F (18/31C)
Open April to October; admission fee
A [R]

Busch Garden
Near Williamsburg, Virginia
Features sections reflecting culture of England, France, and Germany.
Jan.: 32/52F (0/11C); July: 66/92F (19/33C)
Open April/May/September/October, weekends—Memorial Day to Labor Day, daily; admission fee
A [R]

Callaway Gardens
Near Pine Mountain, Georgia
Include 2,500 acres (1,010 hectares) of green meadows, rolling hills, lakes, and woodlands. The gardens offer boating, dining, fishing, golfing, and swimming.
Jan.: 36/62F (2/17C); July: 68/92F (20/33C)
Open year-round; admission fee
[R]

Cape Canaveral
Near Cocoa Beach, Florida
Site of the John F. Kennedy Space Center and the launch site of the first spacecraft to land people on the moon.
Jan.: 52/76F (11/24C); July: 72/92F (22/33C)
Open year-round; admission fee
[R]

Capitols

Jackson, Mississippi

Offer many reminders of the state's rich history. At Old Capitol, Mississippi voted in January 1861 to secede from the Union. Jefferson Davis, president of the Confederacy, made his last speech here in 1884.

Jan.: 36/64F (2/18C); July: 70/94F (21/34C)

Open year-round except major holidays

Cass Scenic Railroad

Cass, West Virginia

State-owned scenic railroad powered by a steam locomotive. Train runs through beautiful mountains.

Jan.: 20/44F (−7/7C); July: 52/80F (11/27C)

Open Memorial Day through Labor Day, Tuesday through Sunday—Labor Day through October, weekends; admission fee

Cherokee, North Carolina

Between Swain and Jackson counties

Includes replica of Oconaluftee Indian village.

Jan.: 26/54F (−3/12C); July: 58/88F (14/31C)

Open year-round; admission fee

Chimney Rock Park

Rutherford County, North Carolina

Rock towers high above the mountains in Rutherford County. Excellent view of Blue Ridge Mountains.

Jan.: 30/54F (−1/12C); July: 62/88F (17/31C)

Open March 1 through November 30; admission fee

Church of the Holy Trinity
Vicksburg, Mississippi
Completed in 1880, has a memorial honoring the Union and Confederate soldiers who fought in the siege of Vicksburg.
Jan.: 36/60F (2/16C); July: 70/94F (21/34C)
Open during spring; tour fee
▲ [R]

Circus World
Near Haines City, Florida
Offers guests opportunities to walk a high wire, fly a trapeze, or be made up like clowns. The theme park also features a thrill ride and a circus musical show.
Jan.: 44/76F (7/24C); July: 72/92F (22/33C)
Open year-round; admission fee
[R]

Constitution Square
Danville, Kentucky
Site where Kentucky's first constitution was adopted in 1792. Visitors may see a restored log courthouse, church, and jail from pioneer days in Kentucky.
Jan.: 26/48F (−3/9C); July: 64/90F (18/32C)
Open year-round
☐

Crater of Diamonds State Park
Near Murfreesboro, Arkansas
Only diamond field in North America. Visitors to mine may hunt for diamonds.
Jan.: 32/56F (0/13C); July: 68/94F (20/34C)
Open year-round; admission fee
▲ [R]

Cypress Gardens
Southeast of Winter Haven, Florida
Tropical gardens and water shows make this one of Florida's leading attractions.
Jan.: 44/76F (7/24C); July: 72/92F (22/33C)
Open year-round; admission fee
[R]

Dahlonega Gold Museum
Dahlonega, Georgia
In 1828, site of the first U.S. gold rush. Visitors can pan for gold at Blackburn State Park.
Jan.: 32/56F (0/13C); July: 60/88F (16/31C)
Open year-round
▲

The Dark Continent/Busch Gardens
Tampa, Florida
Covers 300 acres and contains African animals, rare birds, and tropical plants. Trains and a monorail carry visitors through the area.
Jan.: 44/76F (7/24C); July: 72/92F (22/33C)
Open year-round; admission fee
▲ [R]

De Soto Caverns
Near Childersburg, Alabama
First courtroom in Jackson County. Confederate soldiers mined saltpeter in cave to make gunpowder.
Jan.: 30/56F (–1/13C); July: 66/92F (19/33C)
Open October/November/February/March, weekends—April through September, daily; admission fee
▲ □

Dogpatch USA

Near Harrison, Arkansas

Amusement park named for Al Capp's famous comic-strip community.

Jan.: 24/52F (–4/11C); July: 66/94F (19/34C)

Open May and September, weekends—Memorial Day through late August, daily; admission fee

R

Etowah Mounds

Near Cartersville, Georgia

Built by prehistoric Indians. One of the nation's largest Indian mounds rises 53 feet (16 meters) and covers 3 acres (1.2 hectares). A museum displays relics.

Jan.: 32/56F (0/13C); July: 60/92F (16/33C)

Open year-round

Evangeline Country

South-central Louisiana

Made famous by Henry Wadsworth Longfellow's poem *Evangeline.* The Evangeline Oak, in St. Martinville, marks the legendary spot where some of the Acadians landed after leaving eastern Canada.

Jan.: 42/66F (6/19C); July: 72/94F (22/34C)

Open year-round; admission fee at Evangeline State Park

R

Fair Park
Dallas, Texas
Covers about 200 acres (81 hectares). Home of the State Fair of Texas. Includes Cotton Bowl stadium, Health and Science Museum, State Music Hall, amusement park, recreational areas, livestock exhibition buildings, aquarium, Hall of State, Museum of Natural History, Age of Steam Railroad Exhibit, and Dallas Garden Center.
Jan.: 30/58F (–1/14C); July; 70/98F (21/37C)
Open year-round
[R]

Feliciana Country
Includes parishes of East and West Feliciana, Louisiana
John J. Audubon, the famous painter of birds, made many sketches here. Area has many old plantation homes, several open to the public.
Jan.: 42/66F (6/19C); July: 68/94F (20/34C)
Open year-round; admission fee
[R]

First Capitol of the Confederacy
Montgomery, Alabama
Alabama's present state capitol, where Jefferson Davis took the oath of office in 1861 as president of the Confederate States of America.
Jan.: 38/64F (3/18C); July: 70/92F (21/33C)
Open year-round except Thanksgiving, Christmas, and New Year's Day
[R]

First White House of the Confederacy
Montgomery, Alabama
Home of President and Mrs. Jefferson Davis during the first months of the Confederacy.
Jan.: 38/64F (3/18C); July: 70/92F (21/33C)
Open year-round except Thanksgiving, Christmas, and New Year's Day
[R]

Fontaine House
Memphis, Tennessee
Stately mansion built in 1871. Features elegant Oriental rugs, chandeliers, and mantels.
Jan.: 32/52F (0/11C); July: 68/92F (20/33C)
Open year-round; admission fee

Fort McHenry
Baltimore, Maryland
Where Francis Scott Key wrote the words to "The Star-Spangled Banner."
Jan.: 28/48F (–2/9C); July: 66/88F (19/31C)
Open year-round
[R]

Fort Massachusetts
Ship Island, Mississippi
Union stronghold and prison during the Civil War.
Jan.: 44/64F (7/18C); July: 74/90F (23/32C)
Open April through September; tour fee

Gardens

Near Charleston, South Carolina

Among South Carolina's most beautiful attractions. Near Charleston are the famous Cypress Gardens, Magnolia Gardens, and Middleton Place Gardens. Cypress Gardens include a variety of colorful flowers and several lagoons flanked by cypress trees. Magnolia Gardens feature more than 500 varieties of flowers and trees from many lands. Middleton Place Gardens are the oldest landscaped gardens in the United States. Begun in 1741, they feature azaleas, camellias, and ancient oak trees. The garden area includes exhibits on plantation life of the 1700's and 1800's.

Jan.: 38/62F (3/17C); July: 70/92F (21/33C)

Open year-round; admission fees

[R]

George Read II House

New Castle, Delaware

Built between 1797 and 1804. A notable example of late Georgian architecture.

Jan.: 26/44F (–3/7C); July: 64/88F (18/31C)

Open year-round, admission fee

☐

Grandfather Mountain

Near Linville, North Carolina

Looks like the huge, sleeping face of an old man.

Jan.: 22/46F (–6/8C); July: 58/84F (14/29C)

Open April through mid-November; admission fee

[R]

Grand Isle
At the entrance of Barataria Bay, south of New Orleans, Louisiana
Fishing center. A few descendants of Jean Laffite's pirate crew live in the island's village.
Jan.: 46/70F (8/21C); July: 72/94F (22/34C)
Open year-round

Grand Ole Opry House
Near Nashville, Tennessee
Features weekly performances of country and western music. Located at Opryland USA, an entertainment park.
Jan.: 30/50 (−1/10C); July: 64/92F (18/33C)
Open year-round; admission fee

Hagley Museum
Near Wilmington, Delaware
Covers 185 acres (75 hectares) on Brandywine Creek. Location of Eleuthère Irénée du Pont's first powder mill. The site has exhibit buildings and 21 mills. Uses old displays and modern, push-button exhibits.
Jan.: 26/44F (−3/7C); July: 64/88F (18/31C)
Open year-round except Thanksgiving, Christmas, New Year's; admission fee

Henry Francis du Pont Winterthur Museum
Near Wilmington, Delaware
Has a magnificent collection of Early American furniture. More than a hundred rooms in the museum are furnished in the styles of periods from 1640 to 1840.
Jan.: 26/44F (−3/7C); July: 64/88F (18/31C)
Open year-round; admission fee

Hermitage
Near Nashville, Tennessee
Stately home of President Andrew Jackson.
Jan.: 30/50F (–1/10C); July: 64/92F (18/33C)
Open year-round; admission fee

Historic Forts
Vicinity of Charleston and Charleston Harbor, South Carolina
Fort Moultrie marks site of a brave defense by the colonists against the British during the Revolutionary War. Fort Johnson is where Americans seized tax stamps from the British in 1765.
Jan.: 38/62F (3/17C); July: 70/92F (21/33C)
Open year-round
R

Horse Farms
Around Lexington, Kentucky
Among Kentucky's most interesting sites. Approximately nine farms are open to the public, including Tom Gentry Farm and Spendthrift Farm.
Jan.: 24/48F (–4/9C); July: 62/88F (17/31C)
Visiting hours vary; admission fees

International Wildlife Park
Near Grand Prairie, Texas
A 485-acre (196-hectare) animal preserve where jungle animals roam free. Visitors may drive through area.
Jan.: 30/58F (–1/14C); July: 70/98F (21/37C)
Open late April through September, daily—spring and fall, weekends; admission fee
R

Jackson's Mill
Near Weston, West Virginia
Boyhood home of General Thomas J. "Stonewall" Jackson. In 1921, area became the first state 4-H Club camp.
Jan.: 24/48F (–4/9C); July: 60/88F (16/31C)
Open Memorial Day to Labor Day

Jamestown Festival Park
James River, Virginia
Has reproductions of old James Fort and the three ships that brought the first settlers to Jamestown in 1607.
Jan.: 32/52F (0/11C); July: 66/92F (19/33C)
Open year-round; admission fee

John Pennekamp Coral Reef State Park
Near Key Largo, Florida
First undersea park in the continental United States. Visitors can see the living reef formations by diving underwater or from glass-bottom boats.
Jan.: 60/80F (16/27C); July: 72/92F (22/33C)
Open year-round; admission fee

Liberty Hall
Frankfort, Kentucky
Senator John Brown built this colonial mansion in the 1790's.
Jan.: 24/48F (–4/9C); July: 64/88F (18/31C)
Open year-round; admission fee

Little White House
Warm Springs, Georgia
Home where President Franklin D. Roosevelt died. The house and nearby Franklin D. Roosevelt Museum contain mementos and other personal belongings of Roosevelt.
Jan.: 36/62F (2/17C); July: 68/92F (20/33C)
Open year-round; admission fee
R

Lookout Mountain
At the Moccasin Bend of the Tennessee River near Chattanooga, Tennessee
Rises 2,146 feet (654 meters) above sea level. In November 1863, Union forces won an important victory here in the Battle Above the Clouds.
Jan.: 30/52F (–1/11C); July: 64/90F (18/32C)
Open year-round

Lyndon B. Johnson Library and Museum
Austin, Texas
Contains exhibits related to the Presidency and more than 30 million documents dealing with U.S. domestic policies and foreign relations.
Jan.: 38/64F (3/18C); July: 70/98F (21/37C)
Open year-round
R

Lyndon B. Johnson Space Center
Houston, Texas
Headquarters for all manned spacecraft projects of the National Aeronautics and Space Administration.
Jan.: 46/64F (8/18C); July: 74/90F (23/32C)
Open year-round

MacArthur Park
Little Rock, Arkansas
Honors Douglas MacArthur, supreme commander of Allied Forces in the Southwest Pacific during World War II. Location of Arkansas Arts Center and the Museum of Science and Industry.
Jan.: 32/56F (0/13C); July: 70/94F (21/34C)
Open year-round
[R]

Marineland
Between St. Augustine and Daytona Beach, Florida
World's first oceanarium. Over 100 kinds of marine life live in natural surroundings.
Jan.: 44/72F (7/22C); July: 72/92F (22/33C)
Open year-round; admission fee
[R]

Maryland State House
Annapolis, Maryland
Where George Washington resigned his commission as commander-in-chief of the Continental Army and where the Treaty of Paris was ratified, ending the American Revolutionary War.
Jan.: 28/48F (−2/9C); July: 66/88F (19/31C)
Open year-round except Christmas Day
[R]

Mission San Jose
San Antonio, Texas
Considered the most beautiful Texas mission. Established in 1720, a marvel of Spanish architecture in North America.
Jan.: 38/70F (3/21C); July: 70/98F (21/37C)
Open year-round; admission fee

Mound State Monument

Near Moundville, Alabama

Has 20 of the South's finest Indian mounds.

Jan.: 34/60F (1/16C); July: 66/92F (19/33C)

Open year-round except Christmas Day; admission fee

My Old Kentucky Home

Near Bardstown, Kentucky

Georgian-style home that inspired Stephen Foster to write "My Old Kentucky Home." Built around 1795 and furnished in the style of the early 1800's. Hostesses dress as women did in that period.

Jan.: 26/48F (–3/9C); July: 64/90F (18/32C)

Open March through November, daily—December through February, Tuesday through Sunday; admission fee

Myrtle Beach

Northern Atlantic coast, South Carolina

Probably the state's most famous seaside resort, offers swimming and sunbathing. Other beaches in the state include Cherry Grove, Ocean Drive, Crescent, Atlantic, Windy Hill, Isle of Palms, Folly, Edisto Island, Hunting Island, and Hilton Head Island.

Jan.: 38/62F (3/17C); July: 70/88F (21/31C)—for Myrtle Beach, only.

Open year-round

Natchitoches Country

West-central Louisiana

Includes the oldest town in the Louisiana Territory. A French trader established Natchitoches on the banks of the Cane River in 1714. The area still has much of its early French character.

Jan.: 38/62F (3/17C); July: 68/98F (20/37C)

Open year-round; tour fees

▲ [R]

National Radio Astronomy Observatory

Pocahontas County, West Virginia

Center for the study of radio waves from space. During the summer, visitors may inspect radio telescopes that measure the waves and may view a film about the observatory's work.

Jan.: 20/44F (–7/7C); July: 52/80F (11/27C)

Open mid-June through August, daily—September through October, weekends

▲ [R]

Natural Bridge

South of Lexington, Virginia

Water carved away softer rock and left the hard rock that forms this famous landmark.

Jan.: 24/48F (–4/9C); July: 62/88F (17/31C)

Open year-round; admission fee

[R]

Natural Chimneys

Near Mount Solon, Virginia

Seven rock towers rise over 100 feet (30 meters).

Jan.: 20/44F (–7/7C); July: 54/80F (12/27C)

Open year-round; admission fee

▲

Natural Tunnel
Near Gate City, Virginia
Giant passageway that the waters of Stock Creek cut through the Purcell Ridge. Railroad runs through tunnel, which includes a path for visitors.
Jan.: 28/52F (–2/11C); July: 62/92F (17/33C)
Open April through November

Okefenokee Swamp
Southeastern Georgia
Includes the Okefenokee National Wildlife Refuge. Visitors may explore water trails on guided boat tours.
Jan.: 40/74F (4/23C); July: 68/96F (20/36C)
Open year-round; admission fee

Old Court House
New Castle, Delaware
Became Delaware's first capitol in 1704.
Jan.: 26/44F (–3/7C); July: 64/86F (18/30C)
Open year-round

Ozark Folk Center
Mountain View, Arkansas
Offers craft demonstrations and musical performances by area residents. The complex has a 1,043-seat auditorium, craft shops, restaurant, lodge, and conference center. Private airfield nearby.
Jan.: 24/52F (–4/11C); July: 66/94F (19/34C)
Open May through October; admission fee

Parthenon
Nashville, Tennessee
Built for the 1897 Tennessee Centennial. World's only reproduction of the ancient temple at Athens, Greece. Has casts of the Elgin Marbles, sculptures from the original Parthenon.
Jan.: 30/50F (–1/10C); July: 64/92F (18/33C)
Open year-round; admission fee
□

Petrified Forest
Near Flora, Mississippi
Contains giant stone trees dating back 30 million years. Facilities include nature trail, geological museum, rock and gem shop, and picnic areas.
Jan.: 36/64F (2/18C); July: 70/94F (21/34C)
Open year-round except Christmas Day; admission fee
▲

Railroad Museum
Jackson, Tennessee
Restored home of Casey Jones, railroad hero of the famous folk ballad that describes his fatal ride.
Jan.: 28/52F (–2/11C); July: 64/92F (18/33C)
Open weekends April to October; admission fee

Saint John's Church
Richmond, Virginia
Where Patrick Henry gave his famous call for liberty or death during the Second Virginia Convention in 1775. Building dates from 1741.
Jan.: 28/52F (–2/11C); July: 66/92F (19/33C)
Open March through November
□

Saint Paul's Episcopal Church
Richmond, Virginia
Church of the Confederacy, where Robert E. Lee and Jefferson Davis worshiped. Dates from 1844.
Jan.: 28/52F (–2/11C); July: 66/92F (19/33C)

San Jacinto Monument
East of downtown Houston, Texas
Honors Texans who fought in the Battle of San Jacinto, in which Texas won independence from Mexico. Memorial monument, one of the tallest in the world, rises 570 feet (174 meters). A star that weighs 220 short tons (200 metric tons) rests at the top.
Jan.: 46/64F (8/18C); July: 74/90F (23/32C)
Open year-round

Sea World
Near Orlando, Florida
Features porpoise and killer whale shows. The marine center also has a colorful water fountain show.
Jan.: 44/76F (7/24C); July: 72/96F (22/36C)
Open year-round; admission fee
R

Sequoyah Caverns
Valley Head, Alabama
Contains beautiful rock formations and clear, shining lakes.
Jan.: 30/56F (–1/13C); July: 66/92F (19/33C)
Open year-round except Christmas Day; admission fee
▲ R

Shaker Village at Pleasant Hill
Near Lexington, Kentucky
Old Shaker settlement. The Shakers, a religious group, settled the area in 1805. Visitors to the guest house may climb several stories on a spiral staircase.
Jan.: 26/48F (–3/9C); July: 64/90F (18/32C)
Open year-round; admission fee
R

Six Flags Over Texas
Arlington, Texas
Amusement park that features history of Texas under the flags of Spain, France, Mexico, Republic of Texas, Confederacy, and United States.
Jan.: 30/58F (–1/14C); July: 70/98F (21/37C)
Open March through mid-May and September through November, weekends—mid-May through August, daily; admission fee
▲ R

State House
Dover, Delaware
Delaware's state capitol until 1933. Built in 1792 and now a museum.
Jan.: 28/46F (–2/8C); July: 66/88F (19/31C)
Open year-round
□

United States Frigate *Constellation*
Baltimore, Maryland
First commissioned ship of the U.S. Navy and oldest U.S. warship afloat.
Jan.: 28/48F (–2/9C); July: 66/88F (19/31C)
Open year-round; admission fee
R

United States Naval Academy
Annapolis, Maryland
Established in 1845. One of the country's major service academies.
Jan.: 28/48F (–2/9C); July: 66/88F (19/31C)
Open year-round

U.S.S. *North Carolina* Battleship Memorial
On the Cape Fear River at Wilmington, North Carolina
Tour of famous battleship, which took part in every major Pacific offensive of World War II.
Jan.: 38/62F (3/17C); July: 70/88F (21/31C)
Open year-round; admission fee

Vicksburg National Military Park
Vicksburg, Mississippi
Honors the siege of Vicksburg, a major turning point of the Civil War. Monuments for each state represented in the battle are located at the site of its troops' battle lines in the park.
Jan.: 36/60F (2/16C); July: 70/94F (21/34C)
Open year-round except Christmas Day

Walt Disney World
Near Orlando, Florida
Features an amusement park, a recreation center, a storybook castle, and other attractions. Walt Disney World Epcot Center features displays that explore future technology.
Jan.: 44/76F (7/24C); July: 72/96F (22/36C)
Open year-round; admission fee

Westville
Lumpkin, Georgia
Reconstructed farming village that shows handicrafts and culture of Georgia of the 1850's. Features craft demonstrations.
Jan.: 40/68F (4/20C); July: 68/96F (20/36C)
Open year-round; admission fee

Wright Brothers National Memorial
Near Cape Hatteras, offshore North Carolina
Site where Wilbur and Orville Wright made the world's first powered aircraft flight.
Jan.: 38/58F (3/14C); July: 70/88F (21/31C)
Open year-round; admission fee

Yamacraw Bluff
Savannah, Georgia
Site where James Oglethorpe landed in 1733. The bluff bears the name of the village whose Indians made the first treaty with Oglethorpe.
Jan.: 40/68F (4/20C); July: 68/92F (20/33C)
Open year-round

Zwaanendael Museum
Lewes, Delaware
Modeled after a wing of the town hall in Hoorn, The Netherlands. The museum's exhibits include historic documents, Indian relics, and mementos of seafaring days in southern Delaware.
Jan.: 30/48F (–1/9C); July: 68/86F (20/30C)
Open year-round except federal and state holidays

West

Akaka Falls

Near Hilo on Hawaii Island, Hawaii

Long, slender waterfall on Kolekole stream. The falls plunge over a 442-foot (135-meter) cliff into a wooded gorge.

70's F (20's C) year-round

Open year-round

[R]

Alaska Highway

Dawson Creek, British Columbia, to Delta Junction, Alaska

Extends 1,422 miles (2,288 kilometers). Linking highways go north to Fairbanks, in gold rush country, and south to Anchorage and other cities.

Jan.: –20/12F (–29/–11C); July: 46/76F (8/20C)—approximate for northernmost sector

Open year-round

▲ [R]

Aloha Tower

Honolulu, Hawaii

Rises above the piers where passenger ships dock. From the top, visitors have a fine view of Honolulu.

70's F (20's C) year-round

Open year-round

[R]

Atmospherium-Planetarium
University of Nevada in Reno, Nevada
Shows realistic motion pictures of hurricanes, tornadoes, and various weather conditions.
Jan.: 16/48F (−9/9C); July: 44/92F (7/33C)
Open year-round except Thanksgiving, Christmas, and New Year's Day; admission fee

Balanced Rock
Near Castleford, Idaho
Balloon-shaped rock 40 feet (12 meters) high that rests on a small block of stone.
Jan.: 16/40F (−9/2C); July: 48/96F (9/36C)
Open year-round

Barking Sands
Kauai, Hawaii
Beach sometimes quite dry. At these times the sand, when walked on, makes a sound like a barking dog.
70's F (20's C) year-round
Open year-round

Beartooth Highway
Leads from Red Lodge, Montana, to Yellowstone Park.
Spectacular mountain views from the Beartooth Plateau, 11,000 feet (3,350 meters) high.
Jan.: 0/28F (−18/−2C); July: 40/84F (4/29C)
Open spring through fall

Beehive House
Salt Lake City, Utah
Restored adobe home of Brigham Young. Built in 1855.
Jan.: 8/44F (–13/9C); July: 44/104F (7/40C)
Open year-round
[R]

Bingham Canyon Copper Pit
Near Salt Lake City, Utah
Largest open-pit copper mine in North America, nearly ½ mile (0.8 kilometer) deep and over 2 miles (3 kilometers) across at its widest point.
Jan.: 8/44F (–13/9C); July: 44/104F (7/40C)
Open year-round
▲ [R]

Booneville Dam
Columbia River, Oregon
First major dam on the Columbia River, has a series of fish ladders. In season, salmon and other fish can be seen jumping upstream via the ladders on the way to spawn.
Jan.: 24/48F (–4/9C); July: 48/84F (9/29C)
Open year-round
[R]

Bonneville Salt Flats
Near Wendover, Utah
Famous for its September racing trials. Has 100 square miles (260 square kilometers) of flat salt beds hard as cement.
Jan.: 8/38F (–13/3C); July: 56/104F (13/40C)
Open year-round
▲ [R]

Bowers Mansion
Near Carson City, Nevada
Large, Italian-style home built by "Sandy" Bowers, a silver miner who made a fortune from the Comstock Lode.
Jan.: 16/48F (−9/9C); July: 44/92F (7/33C)
Open Memorial Day through Labor Day; admission fee

Buffalo Bill's Grave
Top of Lookout Mountain near Golden, Colorado
Honors the famous scout and showman William F. Cody (Buffalo Bill).
Jan.: 8/44F (−13/7C); July: 56/96F (13/36C)
Open year-round

Cataldo Mission (Old Mission of the Sacred Heart)
West of Kellogg, Idaho
Idaho's oldest building. Begun in the 1850's by Indians directed by Father Anthony Ravalli, a Roman Catholic missionary. Has been restored as a historical site.
Jan.: 16/28F (−9/−2C); July: 40/80F (4/27C)
Open year-round

Central City, Colorado
Once a rich gold camp, now a summer resort. A theater-and-music festival is held each summer in the old-time opera house.
Jan.: 8/44F (−13/7C); July: 56/96F (13/36C)
Open year-round; admission fee

Church of Tomorrow

Oklahoma City, Oklahoma

Has a 1,500-seat sanctuary, an educational building, and a theater-in-the-round.

Jan.: 26/52F (–3/11C); July: 68/98F (20/37C)

Open year-round

R

Columbia River Gorge

Columbia River, Oregon, where the river cuts through the Cascade Mountains on its way to the Pacific Ocean

Colorful basalt cliffs line the deep gorge for about 60 miles (97 kilometers) between The Dalles and Troutdale. Multnomah and other waterfalls tumble into the gorge.

Jan.: 24/48F (–4/9C); July: 48/84F (19/29C)

Open year-round; fee for boat tour

R

Creek Capitol

Okmulgee, Oklahoma

Building from which Creek Indians ruled their republic.

Jan.: 26/52F (–3/11C); July: 68/94F (20/34C)

Open year-round; admission fee

□

Crystal Ice Cave

Near American Falls, Idaho

Has a frozen river, frozen waterfall, and other formations of ice and stone.

Jan.: 8/32F (–13/0C); July: 48/96F (9/36C)

Open May 1 through October 31; admission fee

□

Disneyland
Anaheim, California
Amusement park designed by Walt Disney. Its attractions include a fairyland castle and a boat trip through "jungle" waters.
Jan.: 40/72F (4/22C); July: 52/88F (11/31C)
Open year-round; admission fee

Fort Sill
Near Lawton, Oklahoma
Military center that includes three historical sites—Stone Corral, Old Guardhouse, and an artillery museum. Fort was established in 1869.
Jan.: 26/56F (−3/13C); July: 68/98F (20/37C)
Open year-round

Garden of the Gods
Near Colorado Springs, Colorado
Breathtaking cluster of huge red sandstone rocks. Thousands of worshipers gather there on Easter Sunday for sunrise services.
Jan.: 8/44F (−13/7C); July: 48/84F (9/29C)
Open year-round

Giant Springs State Park
Near Great Falls, Montana
Giant Springs discharges 270,000 gallons (1,020,000 liters) of water a minute.
Jan.: 8/36F (−13/2C); July: 48/92F (9/33C)
Open year-round

Gila Wilderness
Near Silver City, New Mexico
First U.S. area set aside as a national wilderness. Kept in its natural condition.
Jan.: 16/56F (–9/13C); July: 48/88F (9/31C)
Open year-round

Grand Coulee Dam
West of Spokane, Washington
Largest concrete dam in the United States.
Jan.: 16/36F (–9/2C); July: 48/88F (9/31C)
Open year-round
R

Great Salt Lake
Near Salt Lake City, Utah
Has water three to seven times saltier than any ocean.
Jan.: 8/44F (–13/9C); July: 44/104F (7/40C)
Open year-round
R

Hamakua Coast
Between Hilo and Honokaa, Hawaii Island, Hawaii
Highway winds through sugar cane plantations and around the base of Mauna Kea, Hawaii's highest mountain.
70's F (20's C) year-round
Open year-round
R

Hells Canyon

Snake River south of Lewiston, Idaho

Deepest canyon in the United States. Narrow, but has an average depth of about 1 mile (1.6 kilometers). Greatest depth is 7,900 feet (2,400 meters).

Jan.: 8/36F (– 13/2C); July: 40/96F (4/36C)

Open year-round

Hell's Half Acre

Near Casper, Wyoming

Rugged 320-acre (129-hectare) depression where wind and water created unusual rock gullies, ridges, and towers.

Jan.: 8/32F (– 13/0C); July: 44/88F (7/31C)

Open year-round

R

Hopi Indian Villages

Navajo County, Arizona

Include the 800-year-old settlement of Oraibi, probably the oldest continuously inhabited place in the United States. Cultural center with museum.

Jan.: 12/52F (– 11/11C); July: 48/96F (9/36C)

Open year-round

Kapiolani Park

From Waikiki to Diamond Head, Honolulu, Hawaii

Offers concerts, pageants, zoo. Diamond Head, an extinct volcano, is in the background.

70's F (20's C) year-round

Open year-round

R

Kirkpatrick Center
Oklahoma City, Oklahoma
Two museums and six galleries containing over 2,000 exhibits.
Open year-round; admission fee

Knott's Berry Farm
Buena Park, California
California's oldest amusement park. Features rides, a ghost town, and an Indian village.
Jan.: 40/72F (4/22C); July: 52/88F (11/31C)
Open mid-March through mid-September, daily—mid-September through mid-March, Friday through Tuesday—closed Christmas Day; admission fee

Lake Mead
South of Las Vegas, Nevada
Man-made lake 115 miles (184 kilometers) long. Formed when Hoover Dam was built across the Colorado River. Just minutes away from the "Las Vegas Strip." Recreational areas provide swimming, boating, skiing, fishing, and camping.
Jan.: 32/56F (0/13C); July: 68/108F (20/42C)
Open year-round; admission fee

Lake Tahoe
Southwest of Carson City, Nevada
Lies in the valley of the Sierra Nevada Range, 6,000 feet (1,800 meters) above sea level. Crystal blue water reflects a picture of the mountains in the background. Recreational area offers boating, fishing, backpacking, and snow skiing.
Jan.: 16/48F (−9/9C); July: 44/92F (7/33C)
Open year-round; admission fee

Lewis and Clark Interpretive Center
Near Ilwaco, Washington
Features maps and paintings of the Lewis and Clark Expedition between Missouri and the Pacific coast.
Jan.: 32/52F (0/11C); July: 48/72F (9/22C)
Open year-round
▲ [R]

London Bridge
Lake Havasu City, Arizona
Stone bridge originally built in London, England, during the early 1800's. Its granite stones were disassembled, shipped to the United States, and reassembled in their original form.
Jan.: 36/76F (2/24C); July: 64/120F (18/49C)
Open year-round
▲ [R]

Los Alamos Bradbury Science Hall and Museum
Los Alamos, New Mexico
Shows the development of atomic energy.
Jan.: 8/40F (–13/4C); July: 48/80F (9/27C)
Open year-round
▲ ☐

Marine Highway
From Prince Rupert, British Columbia, to southeastern coastal cities of Alaska
Alaska's state ferryliner system. Ocean-going ferryliners carry cars and passengers. Each town along this scenic route offers special attractions.
Jan.: 20/48F (–7/9C); July: 46/68F (8/20C)
Open year-round
▲ [R]

Marineland of the Pacific
Rancho Palos Verdes, California
World's largest oceanarium. Its aquariums contain sharks, porpoises, and other interesting sea life.
Jan.: 40/72F (4/22C); July: 52/88F (11/31C)
Open May through September, daily—October through April, Saturday through Wednesday; admission fee
▲ [R]

Maryhill Museum
On the Columbia River, Klickitat County, Washington
Art museum in an elaborate mansion that multimillionaire Samuel Hill built in 1926. Gray stone structure stands on high bluff overlooking Columbia River Gorge.
Jan.: 24/44F (−4/7C); July: 48/88F (9/31C)
Open March 15 through November 15; admission fee
▲ [R]

Medicine Rocks State Park
Near Ekalaka, Montana
In the badlands of eastern Montana. Wind and water carved these sandstone rocks into unusual shapes.
Jan.: 0/32F (−18/0C); July: 56/92F (13/33C)
Open year-round
▲ [R]

Meteor Crater
Coconino County, Arizona
Large hole formed after a huge object from space struck the earth and went so deep it has never been located.
Jan.: 12/52F (−11/11C); July: 48/96F (9/36C)
Open year-round; admission fee
[R]

Monterey Peninsula

Includes Carmel, Monterey, Pacific Grove, and Pebble Beach, California

Carmel is a famous art colony. Monterey has buildings dating from Spanish colonial days. Sights along the Seventeen-Mile Drive between Pacific Grove and Carmel include rocks with seals and Pebble Beach Golf Course. Some wineries in the area are open to the public.

Jan.: 32/64F (0/18C); July: 44/88F (7/31C)

Open year-round

[R]

Monument Valley

Southeastern Utah

Has red sandstone formations that rise 1,000 feet (300 meters). In the evening, formation called the *totem pole* casts a shadow 35 miles (56 kilometers) long.

Jan.: 16/52F (−9/11C); July: 56/104F (13/40C)

Open year-round

□

Narrow Gauge Railroad

Between Durango and Silverton, Colorado

One of the last passenger railroads of its type in the country. The tracks of the railroad are set closer together than modern ones. In summer, visitors can take a 90-mile (140-kilometer) round trip on the train through beautiful canyons.

Jan.: 16/44F (−9/7C); July: 56/96F (13/36C)

Open year-round; tour fee

[R]

National Cowboy Hall of Fame and Western Heritage Center
Oklahoma City, Oklahoma
Famous paintings and sculptures on display.
Jan.: 26/52F (–3/11C); July: 68/98F (20/37C)
Open year-round; admission fee
[R]

National Elk Refuge
Near Jackson, Wyoming
Largest of the state's major wildlife refuge areas. Animals and birds live in natural surroundings.
Jan.: 0/32F (–18/0C); July: 36/80F (2/27C)
Open year-round
[R]

Nuuanu Pali
Upper end of Nuuanu Valley on Oahu, Hawaii
Offers a magnificent view of the northeastern coast from a cliff 1,188 feet (362 meters) high. A highway leads to the top of the cliff. King Kamehameha I drove some of Oahu's defenders over this cliff when he conquered the island in 1795.
70's F (20's C) year-round
Open year round

Old Fort Hall
Pocatello, Idaho
Reconstruction of a trading post that became an important stop in Idaho on the Oregon Trail. Original fort was built in 1834.
Jan.: 8/32F (–13/0C); July: 48/96F (9/36C)
Open April through September
□

Old Nevada

West of Las Vegas, Nevada

Full-scale town depicting life in Nevada during the "boom days." Has 45 authentic buildings.

Jan.: 24/56F (–4/13C); July: 60/100F (16/38C)

Open year-round; admission fee

R

Painted Desert

Along the Little Colorado River, northern Arizona

Extends about 200 miles (320 kilometers). A brilliantly colored region with buttes, mesas, pinnacles, and valleys formed by ages of wind and rain cutting into shalelike volcanic ash.

Jan.: 12/52F (–11/11C); July: 48/108F (9/42C)

Open year-round

R

Pearl Harbor

Oahu, Hawaii

Huge natural harbor used as a U.S. naval base. The battleship *Arizona*, sunk in the Japanese attack of December 7, 1941, rests on the harbor bottom.

70's F (20's C) year-round

Open year-round

R

Philmont Scout Ranch

Headquarters near Cimarron, New Mexico

A 137,000-acre (55,440-hectare) Boy Scout recreational area and a working ranch. Headquarters has a museum.

Jan.: 8/48F (–13/9C); July: 48/88F (9/31C)

Open mid-June to late August

Picture Gorge
Near Dayville, Oregon
Canyon of basalt rock named for Indian pictures on the walls. John Day Fossil Beds National Monument has fossils of prehistoric animals and plants.
Jan.: 12/40F (–11/4C); July: 48/92F (9/33C)
Open year-round

Pikes Peak
West of Colorado Springs, Colorado
Probably the most famous mountain in the Rockies. Visitors can reach the top by automobile toll road or cog railway, on horseback or on foot.
Jan.: 8/44F (–13/7C); July: 48/84F (9/29C)
Open year-round; admission fee
▲ [R]

Point Barrow, Alaska
Northernmost point in Alaska, 300 miles (482 kilometers) above the Arctic Circle. Eskimos follow old ways of life. In midsummer, the "midnight sun" glows all night.
Jan.: –30/–6F (–34/–21C); July: 34/52F (1/11C)
Open in summer
$ [R]

Polynesian Cultural Center
Near Laie on Oahu, Hawaii
Includes six Polynesian villages inhabited by people from Fiji, Tonga, Hawaii, New Zealand, Samoa, and Tahiti.
70's F (20's C) year-round
Open year-round; admission fee
$ [R]

Puyé Cliff Dwellings
West of Española, New Mexico
Ancient Indian "apartment houses."
Jan.: 8/40F (–13/4C); July: 48/80F (9/27C)
Open year-round; admission fee
□

Redwood Highway
U.S. 101, from San Francisco, California, to Oregon
Passes through magnificent groves of redwood, the tallest trees in the world.
Jan.: 32/56F (0/13C); July: 44/88F (7/31C)
Open year-round
[R]

Rocky Reach Dam
Near Wenatchee, Washington
Has museum and underground room where visitors can watch salmon swim upstream to spawn.
Jan.: 16/36F (–9/2C); July: 48/88F (9/31C)
Open year-round
[R]

Royal Gorge
Near Canon City, Colorado
Massive canyon cut by the Arkansas River. The gorge, more than 1,000 feet (300 meters) deep, is crossed by the world's highest suspension bridge.
Jan.: 16/52F (–9/11C); July: 56/96F (13/36C)
Open year-round; admission fee
[R]

Ruins of Indian Cliff Dwellings

Near Blanding, Utah

Cliff dwellings believed to have housed Anasazi Indians, who lived hundreds of years ago in what is now Utah. Other ancient dwellings may be found in Bluff, Kanab, Moab, Parowan, Price, and Vernal, Utah.

Jan.: 8/44F (– 13/9C); July: 44/104F (7/40C)

Open year-round

San Diego Zoo

San Diego, California

Has the largest collection of birds, mammals, and reptiles in the world. Its monkey and ape exhibits rank among the finest in North America.

Jan.: 40/72F (4/22C); July: 44/88F (7/31C)

Open year-round; admission fee

R

San Juan Islands

Washington State, near Canada's Vancouver Island

Vacation resorts noted for their scenic beauty.

Jan.: 24/52F (– 4/11C); July: 48/80F (9/27C)

Open year-round; ferry fee

R

San Miguel Mission

Santa Fe, New Mexico

Built by the Spaniards in 1626 and restored in 1710.

Jan.: 8/48F (– 13/9C); July: 40/80F (4/27C)

Open year-round

R

San Simeon
Near San Luis Obispo, California
Former estate of newspaper owner William Randolph Hearst. Includes a castle with ancient works of art, a Roman temple, a private theater, huge swimming pools, and landscaped gardens.
Jan.: 40/72F (4/22C); July: 44/88F (7/31C)
Open year-round; admission fee; reservations advisable.
[R]

San Xavier del Bac Mission
Near Tucson, Arizona
Probably the best preserved of Arizona's early missions. Has many beautiful and unusual carvings and paintings.
Jan. 24/64F (–4/18C); July: 64/108F (18/42C)
Open year-round

Sea Life Park
Makapuu Point on Oahu, Hawaii
Scientific and recreational oceanarium with performing porpoises and whales.
70's F (20's C) year-round
Open year-round; admission fee
[R]

Sea Lion Caves
On the Pacific coast near Florence, Oregon
Home of hundreds of sea lions.
Jan.: 36/56F (2/13C); July: 48/76F (9/24C)
Open year-round; admission fee
[R]

Seattle Center
Seattle, Washington
Includes the Pacific Science Center from the Century 21 Exposition, a world's fair held in 1962. Space Needle, a nearby tower 607 feet (185 meters) high, has observation deck. Monorail links the center and downtown Seattle.
Jan.: 32/52F (0/11C); July: 48/80F (9/27C)
Open year-round; admission fee
R

Shoshone Falls
Near Twin Falls, Idaho
A 212-foot (65-meter) waterfall in Snake River Canyon.
Jan.: 8/40F (–13/4C); July: 48/96F (9/36C)
Open year-round

Shoshone Ice Caves
Near Shoshone, Idaho
Under lava fields. Ice covers caves' walls and ceilings.
Jan.: 8/36F (–13/2C); July: 48/96F (9/36C)
Open year-round; admission fee

Silver City
Owyhee County, Idaho
Mining ghost town with restored hotel, school, and other buildings, plus cemetery and mines. Bus transportation available in summer.
Jan.: 8/40F (–13/4C); July: 48/88F (9/31C)
Open spring, summer, fall; check locally for road conditions

Thomas Gilcrease Institute of American History and Art
Tulsa, Oklahoma
Art gallery and library. Contains over 5,000 works of art, including many paintings on the American West's history.
Jan.: 26/52F (–3/11C); July: 68/94F (20/34C)
Open year-round
R

Tombstone
Cochise County, Arizona
Famous Western boom town where Wyatt Earp won fame as a gunfighter.
Jan.: 24/64F (–4/18C); July: 48/96F (9/36C)
Open year-round
R

Trolley Square
Salt Lake City, Utah
Colorful center of restaurants and shops in renovated trolley car barns.
Jan.: 8/44F (–13/9C); July: 44/104F (7/40C)
Open year-round
R

Tsa-La-Gi Indian Village
Southeast of Tahlequah, Oklahoma
Re-creates an ancient Cherokee village. Cherokee give tours of village.
Jan.: 26/52F (–3/11C); July: 68/94F (20/34C)
Open early May through late August; admission fee

United States Air Force Academy
North of Colorado Springs, Colorado
Trains the U.S. Air Force's officers. The Visitors Center at the south entrance shows films about the academy.
Jan.: 8/44F (–13/7C); July: 48/84F (9/29C)
Open year-round

United States Mint
Denver, Colorado
Makes millions of coins each year. Tours available.
Jan.: 8/44F (–13/7C); July: 56/96F (13/36C)
Open year-round

Virginia City
Near Dillon, Montana
Restored to look the way the town did in 1865, when it was one of the nation's richest gold camps.
Jan.: 0/28F (–18/–2C); July: 40/84F (4/29C)
Open mid-June through Labor Day

Virginia City
Southeast of Reno, Nevada
Silver mined in Virginia City helped to finance the Civil War for the Union and build a large part of San Francisco. Many original buildings are still intact.
Jan.: 16/48F (–9/9C); July: 44/92F (7/33C)
Open year-round; admission fee

Will Rogers Memorial
Claremore, Oklahoma
Contains paintings, manuscripts, and other personal belongings of the Oklahoma-born humorist.
Jan.: 26/52F (–3/11C); July: 68/94F (20/34C)
Open year-round
□

Wind River Canyon
South of Thermopolis, Wyoming
Offers motorists a scenic drive between the Bridger and Owl Creek mountains. Cliffs rise 2,000 feet (610 meters) above river. Rock formations exposed where river cut through mountains.
Jan.: –8/40F (–22/5C); July: 52/96F (11/36C)
Open year-round
▲ [R]

Woolaroc Museum
Southwest of Bartlesville, Oklahoma
Displays over 55,000 historical exhibits, many dealing with Southwest history. Includes paintings of Frederic Remington and Charles Russell.
Jan.: 22/48F (–6/7C); July: 68/94F (20/34C)
Open year-round
[R]

Yuma Territorial Prison State Historic Park
Yuma, Arizona
"Hell Hole" of Arizona, a prison built in 1875. Museum, old cell blocks, dungeon.
Jan.: 36/76F (2/24C); July: 80/120F (27/49C)
Open year-round
[R]

Canada

Barbour's General Store
St. John, New Brunswick
Restored country store dating from mid-1800's. Shelves contain merchandise of this period.
Jan.: 0/30F (–18/–1C); July: 50/75F (10/24C)
Open mid-May through mid-October
▲ R

Barkerville
Cariboo Mountains, east-central British Columbia
Restored gold rush town. A museum features items from gold rush days. Can be reached by the Cariboo Highway, a historic trail through rugged canyon country in the Cariboo Mountains.
Jan.: 5/24F (–15/–4C); July: 40/80F (4/27C)
Open year-round
▲ R

Bell Homestead
Brantford, Ontario
Home of inventor of the telephone, Alexander Graham Bell, who worked on his invention there in 1874. Now a telephone museum. Contains the Bell Memorial, a huge stone sculpture of the inventor.
Jan.: 10/40F (–12/4C); July: 55/85F (13/29C)
Open year-round
▲ R

Bluenose II
Halifax Harbor, Nova Scotia
Replica of *Bluenose*, a Canadian racing schooner that won the International Fisherman's Trophy in 1921–1923, 1926, and 1938. Visitors may tour *Bluenose II* when the ship is in port.
Jan.: 10/30F (– 12/ – 1C); July: 50/75F (10/24C)
Open July and August

Bonaventure Island
Off the Gaspé Peninsula near Percé, Quebec
One of the largest water-bird refuges open to the public. More than 60,000 gannets, gulls, and other birds nest on the island in summer.
Jan.: 0/20F (– 18/ – 7C); July: 5/75F (10/24C)
Open year-round
R

Cabot Trail
Northern Cape Breton Island, Nova Scotia
Highway winding through wilderness areas. Magnificent view of the sea.
Jan.: 10/40F (– 12/4C); July: 50/75F (10/24C)
Open year-round
R

Cape Blomidon
Near Wolfville, Nova Scotia
Overlooks Minas Basin and nearby apple orchards.
Jan.: 10/30F (– 12/ – 1C); July: 55/80F (13/27C)
Open year-round

Columbia Ice Field
Between Banff and Jasper, Alberta
Consists of huge glaciers from the Ice Age. Tourists ride in snowmobiles over Athabasca Glacier, part of the ice field.
Jan.: 0/20F (−18/−7C); July: 40/75F (4/24C)
Open year-round

Confederation Chamber
Province House in Charlottetown, Prince Edward Island
Called the *Birthplace of Canada*. Furnished as it was in 1864, when the Fathers of Confederation first met there and planned the union of Canada.
Jan.: 10/20F (−12/−7C); July: 65/70F (18/21C)
Open year-round

Covered Bridge
Over the St. John River in Hartland, New Brunswick
Covered bridge 1,282 feet (391 meters) long. Believed to be longest covered bridge in the world.
Jan.: 0/30F (−18/−1C); July: 55/80F (13/27C)
Open year-round

Dawson City
Mouth of the Klondike River, Yukon Territory
Boom town during Klondike Gold Rush in 1897 and 1898. Includes many landmarks of era.
Jan.: −16F (−27C); July: 60F (16C)
Open year-round

Fort Macleod, Alberta
Has a full-size replica of the Alberta region's first North-West Mounted Police post, established in 1874. Museum dealing with the history of the Mounties.
Jan.: 0/30F (–18/–1C); July: 45/80F (7/27C)
Open May through October; admission fee
R

Fort Steele
Near Cranbrook, British Columbia
Reconstruction of a town in the East Kootenay District in the 1890's. Has a museum and a steam railroad.
Jan.: 0/30F (–18/–1C); July: 45/80F (7/27C)
Open year-round
R

Frank Slide
Near Sentinel, southwestern Alberta
Site of a 1903 landslide. The top of Turtle Mountain crashed down into Crowsnest Pass, buried part of the town of Frank, and killed about 70 persons.
Jan.: 0/30F (–18/–1C); July: 45/80F (7/27C)
Open year-round
R

Gander Airport
Gander, Newfoundland
Once a strategic terminal for air travel between North America and Europe. Includes exhibit of transatlantic aviation.
Jan.: 10/30F (–12/–1C); July: 50/70F (10/21C)
Open year-round
R

Horseshoe Falls
Near the Ontario-New York border
Largest part of Niagara Falls, 2,600 feet (790 meters) wide and 158 feet (48 meters) high.
Jan.: 0/30F (−18/−1C); July: 55/85F (13/29C)
Open year-round
R

Île d'Orléans (Montmorency II County)
Near Quebec City, Quebec
About 4,500 French Canadians live on the island, which rises in the middle of the St. Lawrence River. Has Norman-style houses, churches, shrines.
Jan.: 0/20F (−18/−7C); July: 55/85F (13/29C)
Open year-round
R

Inside Passage to Alaska
From Seattle, Washington, and Vancouver, British Columbia, to Prince Rupert and on to Juneau and other Alaskan ports. One of the most scenic water routes in the world.
Jan.: 20/50F (−7/10C); July: 50/80F (10/27C)—Vancouver area only
Open late May through September

International Peace Garden
In Manitoba and North Dakota
Honors the long friendship between Canada and the United States. Memorial made of rocks from both countries marks the international boundary.
Jan.: −20/20F (−29/−7C); July: 50/85F (10/29C)
Open year-round; admission fee
R

Jack Miner's Bird Sanctuary
Kingsville, Ontario
Dedicated to the memory of the famous Ontario naturalist. Covers 300 acres (120 hectares).
Jan.: 10/40F (–12/4C); July: 60/85F (16/29C)
Open October through mid-April
▲ [R]

Keillor House
Dorchester, New Brunswick
Large stone house built in 1813. Has nine working fireplaces and 1800's furnishings.
Jan.: 0/30F (–18/–1C); July: 50/80F (10/27C)
Open year-round; admission fee
[R]

Kings Landing Historical Settlement
Prince William, New Brunswick
Restored village that shows how the people in the region lived during the 1800's. Established after the American Revolutionary War by the Kings American Dragoons, a unit of the Royal Provincial Army that aided the British Army.
Jan.: 0/30F (–18/–1C); July: 55/80F (13/27C)
Open late May to Labor Day; admission fee
▲ [R]

Lennox Island
Malpeque Bay, Prince Edward Island
Has a Micmac Indian reservation. Malpeque Bay also has the island's chief oyster farms.
Jan.: 10/20F (–12/–7C); July: 65/70F (18/21C)
Open mid-June through mid-September
▲ □

Lighthouse Route
Between Yarmouth and Halifax, Nova Scotia
Passes many interesting small fishing villages.
Jan.: 10/30F (–12/–1C); July: 50/75F (10/24C)
Open year-round

Magnetic Hill
Near Moncton, New Brunswick
Offers a remarkable optical illusion. An automobile, left in neutral gear near what appears to be the bottom of the hill, will seemingly roll uphill to the top.
Jan.: 0/30F (–18/–1C); July: 50/80F (10/27C)
Open year-round

Man and His World
Montreal, Quebec
International cultural exhibition, a continuation of Expo 67. Several countries represented.
Jan.: 0/30F (–18/–1C); July: 55/85F (13/29C)
Open mid-June through October; admission fee

Manitoba Agricultural and Homesteader Village
Austin, Manitoba
Has one of Canada's largest collections of steam engines, as well as gasoline tractors and other antique farm equipment. Also includes a reconstructed pioneer village.
Jan.: –20/10F (–29/–12C); July: 50/85F (10/29C)
Open May through October; admission fee

Manitoulin Island
Lake Huron, Ontario
Probably the world's largest freshwater island, 90 miles (140 kilometers) long and 5 to 30 miles (8 to 48 kilometers) wide. Covers 1,068 square miles (2,766 square kilometers).
Jan.: 0/30F (–18/–1C); July: 50/80F (10/27C)
Open late April through mid-October; ferry fee
[R]

Micmac Indian Village
Near Rocky Point, Prince Edward Island
Reproduction of a 1700's Indian settlement.
Jan.: 10/20F (–12/–7C); July: 65/70F (18/21C)
Open mid-May through early October; admission fee
[R]

Moose Jaw Wild Animal Park
Moose Jaw, Saskatchewan
Largest park of its kind in Saskatchewan. Has lions, monkeys, and many animals from province.
Jan.: –10/20F (–23/–7C); July: 50/85F (10/29C)
Open May through September
[R]

Mount Royal Park
Montreal, Quebec
Lovely wooded area. Only horse-drawn vehicles are allowed in most of park. Top of Mount Royal, 763 feet (233 meters) high, offers magnificent view of Montreal and the St. Lawrence.
Jan.: 0/30F (–18/–1C); July: 55/85F (13/29C)
Open year-round
[R]

Nikka Yuko
Lethbridge, Alberta
Large, authentic Japanese garden. Japanese hostesses in traditional costumes welcome visitors to this setting of specially arranged flowers, rocks, and shrubs.
Jan.: 0/30F (−18/−1C); July: 50/85F (10/29C)
Open Victoria Day weekend through Thanksgiving weekend, daily; admission fee

North Lake
Near Elmira, Prince Edward Island
Known as the tuna-fishing capital of the world.
Jan.: 10/20F (−12/−7C); July: 65/70F (18/21C)
Open year-round

Norway House
Northern end of Lake Winnipeg, Manitoba
Built in 1826, this old Hudson's Bay Company post has many articles from fur-trading days.
Jan.: −30/−10F (−34/−23C); July: 40/65F (4/18C)
Open year-round

Ontario Place
Toronto, Ontario
Cultural and recreational complex lying on artificially created islands in Lake Ontario. Features concerts, movie theater, and facilities for boating and picnics.
Jan.: 10/30F (−12/−1C); July: 55/80F (13/27C)
Open mid-May to Labor Day; admission fee

Placentia

In Castle Hill National Historic Park on the west coast of the Avalon Peninsula, Newfoundland

Established by the French in 1662. Prime Minister Winston Churchill and President Franklin D. Roosevelt drew up the Atlantic Charter on a warship near Placentia in 1941.

Jan.: 10/40F (–12/4C); July: 50/65F (10/18C)

Open June through October

[R]

Port de Grave

Conception Bay, Newfoundland

One of Newfoundland's most scenic areas. Attracts many artists and photographers.

Jan.: 10/30F (–12/–1C); July: 50/70F (10/21C)

Open year-round

Queen Elizabeth Park

Vancouver, British Columbia

On a hill, offers excellent views of the city on clear days. Park has an arboretum with a beautiful sunken garden.

Jan.: 20/50F (–7/10C); July: 50/80F (10/27C)

Open year-round

[R]

Red River Valley

Near Winnipeg, Manitoba

Site of first Manitoba colony. Historic houses and stone churches dot valley's prairies and grain fields.

Jan.: –20/10F (–29/–12C); July: 55/80F (13/27C)

Open May to October, daily—winter months, weekends; admission fee

Roosevelt Summer Home and Park, Campobello
Campobello Island in the Bay of Fundy, New Brunswick
Site of President Franklin D. Roosevelt's summer house.
Jan.: 0/30F (–18/–1C); July: 50/75F (10/24C)
Open mid-May through mid-October, daily
R

Royal Canadian Mounted Police Training Center
Regina, Saskatchewan
Mounties' training headquarters. Has museum of historic documents, uniforms, and weapons.
Jan.: –20/20F (–29/–7C); July: 50/85F (10/29C)
Open year-round
R

Souris, Prince Edward Island
Home port of many commercial fishing boats. Provides facilities for deep-sea fishing.
Jan.: 10/20F (–12/–7C); July: 65/70F (18/21C)
Open year-round
R

Sunrise Trail
Northumberland Strait between Amherst and the Strait of Canso, Nova Scotia
Highway runs along the shore for 212 miles (341 kilometers).
Jan.: 0/40F (–18/4C); July: 50/80F (10/27C)
Open year-round
R

The Pas
Northwest of Cedar Lake, Manitoba
Historic northern crossroads town. Its name came from the Cree Indian word *opas*, or "narrows." Site of the Little Northern Museum.
Jan.: –20/10F (–29/–12C); July: 50/80F (10/27C)
Open Saturday through Wednesday—closed during Christmas season
[R]

Thunderbird Park
Victoria, British Columbia
Has examples of Indian art. Its collection of totem poles,with others in the Provincial Museum, form the finest group in existence.
Jan.: 20/50F (–7/10C); July: 50/80F (10/27C)
Open year-round
[R]

Western Development Museum
Saskatoon, Saskatchewan
Has collection of antique cars, pioneer household equipment, and steam engines.
Jan.: –20/10F (–29/–12C); July: 50/80F (10/27C)
Open year-round
[R]

Witless Bay
South of St. John's, Newfoundland
Small fishing village that offers boat trips to sea-bird nesting colonies on offshore islands.
Jan.: 10/30F (–12/–1C); July: 50/70F (10/21C)
Open year-round

United States and Canadian national park systems

United States national parks

Acadia* (Maine) Highest land on Atlantic Coast of the United States; rugged coastline

Arches* (Utah) Giant rock arches, windows, and towers formed by erosion

Badlands*† (South Dakota) Rugged ravines, ridges, and cliffs; prehistoric animal fossils

Big Bend*† (Texas) Chisos Mountains and Desert in big bend of Rio Grande

Biscayne* (Florida) Living coral reef in Atlantic Ocean and Biscayne Bay

Bryce Canyon*† (Utah) Oddly shaped, beautifully colored rock formations in horseshoe-shaped basins

Canyonlands* (Utah) Canyons, mesas, and sandstone spires; 1,000-year-old Indian rock carvings

Capitol Reef* (Utah) Colorful ridge 60 miles (97 kilometers) long with white dome-shaped rock

Carlsbad Caverns (New Mexico) Huge underground caves with strange rock formations

Channel Islands* (California) Large sea lion breeding place; nesting sea birds; animal fossils

Crater Lake *† (Oregon) Lake in dead volcano; colorful lava walls almost 2,000 feet (610 meters) high

Denali*† (Alaska) Mt. McKinley, highest mountain in North America; wildlife

Everglades*† (Florida) Subtropical wilderness with plentiful wildlife

Gates of the Arctic (Alaska) Jagged peaks, gentle arctic valleys, wild rivers, and numerous lakes

Glacier*† (Montana) Many glaciers and lakes among towering Rocky Mountain peaks

Glacier Bay*† (Alaska) Glaciers that move down mountainsides and break up into the sea; much wildlife

Grand Canyon*† (Arizona) Canyon 1 mile (1.6 kilometers) deep with brightly colored walls and rock shapes

Grand Teton*† (Wyoming) Rugged Teton peaks; winter feeding ground of large elk herd

Great Smoky Mountains*† (North Carolina, Tennessee) High mountains; large hardwood and evergreen forests

Guadalupe Mountains* (Texas) Fossil limestone reef; evergreen forest overlooking desert

Haleakala* (Hawaii) Inactive volcano with large, colorful crater

Hawaii Volcanoes*† (Hawaii) Two active volcanoes; rare plants and animals

Hot Springs* (Arkansas) Mineral springs at base of Hot Springs Mountain

Isle Royale*†‡ (Michigan) Island wilderness with large moose herd and wolves

Katmai* (Alaska) Valley of Ten Thousand Smokes, scene of 1912 volcanic eruption

Kenai Fiords (Alaska) The Harding Icefield, one of the major icecaps in the United States

Kings Canyon*† (California) Mountain wilderness of giant sequoia trees

Kobuk Valley† (Alaska) Rich in arctic wildlife, including caribou, bears, and wolves; archeological sites

Lake Clark† (Alaska) Jagged peaks, granite spires, glaciers, and two active volcanoes

Lassen Volcanic*† (California) Dormant volcano; steep domes of lava

Mammoth Cave*† (Kentucky) Huge cave with 212 miles (341 kilometers) of corridors; underground lakes, rivers, and waterfalls

Mesa Verde*† (Colorado) Prehistoric Indian cliff dwellings

Mount Rainier*† (Washington) Greatest single-peak glacier system in United States

North Cascades* (Washington) Mountain wilderness with glaciers, lakes, waterfalls, and jagged peaks

Olympic*† (Washington) Oceanside mountain wilderness with rain forest and elk

Petrified Forest (Arizona) Ancient, rock-hard wood; Indian ruins; Painted Desert

Redwood* (California) World's tallest known tree in coastal redwood forest

Rocky Mountain* (Colorado) More than 100 peaks over 11,000 feet (3,350 meters) high

Sequoia*† (California) Giant sequoia trees; Mount Whitney

Shenandoah*† (Virginia) Blue Ridge Mountains; hardwood forest; Skyline Drive

Theodore Roosevelt* (North Dakota) Badlands along Little Missouri River and part of President Theodore Roosevelt's ranch

Virgin Islands*† (Virgin Islands) White beaches; tropical plants and animals

Voyageurs*† (Minnesota) Beautiful northern forests of aspen, birch, pine, and spruce; more than 50 lakes

Wind Cave* (South Dakota) Limestone caverns; prairie wildlife

Wrangell-St. Elias*† (Alaska) Country's largest collection of glaciers and peaks over 16,000 feet (4,877 meters)

Yellowstone*† (Idaho, Montana, Wyoming) World's greatest geyser area; canyons and waterfalls; wide variety of wildlife

Yosemite*† (California) Mountain scenery with deep gorges and high waterfalls

Zion*† (Utah) Colorful canyons and mesas

*Camping permitted. †Has overnight lodging. ‡Closed part of year.

United States national historic sites

Abraham Lincoln Birthplace (Kentucky) Log cabin inside memorial building on site of Lincoln's birthplace

Adams (Massachusetts) Home of Adams family, including Presidents John Adams and John Quincy Adams

Allegheny Portage Railroad (Pennsylvania) Honors Pennsylvania Canal and the railroad that carried canal boat passengers and cargoes over Allegheny Mountains

Andersonville (Georgia) Confederate prison camp during Civil War

Andrew Johnson (Tennessee) President Andrew Johnson's home, tailor shop, and grave

Bent's Old Fort (Colorado) Important fur-trading post of Old West

Carl Sandburg Home (North Carolina) The poet's home and farm

Christiansted (Virgin Islands) Honors Danish colonial development of Virgin Islands

Clara Barton (Maryland) Home of Clara Barton, founder of the American Red Cross

Edgar Allan Poe (Pennsylvania) Home of American poet and short-story writer Edgar Allan Poe

Edison (New Jersey) Laboratories and home of inventor Thomas A. Edison

Eisenhower* (Pennsylvania) Home and farm of Dwight D. Eisenhower during and after his presidency

Eleanor Roosevelt* (New York) Val-Kill estate built for first lady by her husband

Eugene O'Neill (California) Home of American playwright Eugene O'Neill

Ford's Theatre (District of Columbia) Ford's Theatre, where President Lincoln was shot, and the nearby house where he died; Lincoln Museum

Fort Bowie (Arizona) Military headquarters for operations against Geronimo and his Apaches

Fort Davis (Texas) Major fort in west Texas defense system against Apaches and Comanches

Fort Laramie (Wyoming) Major post that guarded covered wagons going west

Fort Larned (Kansas) Protection of Santa Fe Trail

Fort Point (California) Brick and granite fort of mid-1800's

Fort Raleigh (North Carolina) Site of first attempted English settlement in what is now United States, in 1585

Fort Scott (Kansas) Commemorates historic events of Civil War period

Fort Smith (Arkansas, Oklahoma) One of first U.S. military posts in Louisiana Territory

Fort Union Trading Post (Montana, North Dakota) Major fur-trading post in upper Missouri River region

Fort Vancouver (Washington) Western headquarters of Hudson's Bay Company

Frederick Law Olmsted* (Massachusetts) Home of Frederick Law Olmsted, park planner of the 1800's

Friendship Hill (Pennsylvania) Home of Albert Gallatin, Secretary of the Treasury under President Thomas Jefferson

Georgia O'Keeffe (New Mexico) Home and studio of American artist Georgia O'Keeffe

Golden Spike (Utah) Honors completion in 1869 of first coast-to-coast railroad system in United States

Grant-Kohrs Ranch (Montana) One of the largest range ranches of 1800's

Hampton (Maryland) Great mansion built in late 1700's

Herbert Hoover (Iowa) Birthplace, boyhood home, and burial place of President Hoover

Home of Franklin D. Roosevelt (New York) Birthplace, home, "Summer White House," and burial place of President Franklin D. Roosevelt

Hopewell Village (Pennsylvania) Rural iron-making village of 1800's

Hubbell Trading Post (Arizona) Shows role of Indian reservation traders in settling West

James A. Garfield (Ohio) Former estate of President Garfield

Jefferson National Expansion Memorial (Missouri) Museum and Gateway Arch 630 feet (192 meters) high honor U.S. expansion west of Mississippi River

John Fitzgerald Kennedy (Massachusetts) Birthplace and early boyhood home of President John F. Kennedy

John Muir (California) Honors contributions to conservation and literature by explorer-naturalist

Knife River Indian Villages (North Dakota) Five Hidatsa Indian villages of 1845

Lincoln Home (Illinois) Only private home owned by Abraham Lincoln

Longfellow (Massachusetts) Home of American poet Henry Wadsworth Longfellow

Maggie L. Walker (Virginia) Home of Maggie L. Walker, a black leader and the first woman president of an American bank

Martin Luther King, Jr. (Georgia) Birthplace, church, and burial place of Martin Luther King, Jr.

Martin Van Buren† (New York) Home of President Martin Van Buren

Ninety Six (South Carolina) Colonial trading post held briefly by the British during the Revolutionary War

Palo Alto Battlefield (Texas) Site of one of two Mexican War battles fought on U.S. soil

Puukohola Heiau (Hawaii) Ruins of a temple built by King Kamehameha I, first ruler of the kingdom of Hawaii

Sagamore Hill (New York) Last home of President Theodore Roosevelt

Saint-Gaudens† (New Hampshire) Home, studio, and gardens of sculptor Augustus Saint-Gaudens

Salem Maritime (Massachusetts) Derby Wharf and other important structures in New England

San Juan (Puerto Rico) Spanish fort begun in 1539 to protect Bay of San Juan

Saugus Iron Works (Massachusetts) One of first ironworks in North America, built in 1640's

Sewall-Belmont House (District of Columbia) Headquarters of National Woman's Party

Springfield Armory (Massachusetts) Produced small arms, such as the Springfield rifle, for nearly 200 years

Theodore Roosevelt Birthplace (New York) Birthplace of 26th President

Theodore Roosevelt Inaugural (New York) House where Theodore Roosevelt was sworn in as President

Thomas Stone* (Maryland) Home of Thomas Stone, a signer of the Declaration of Independence

Tuskegee Institute (Alabama) Student-made college buildings; home of Booker T. Washington; George Washington Carver Museum

Vanderbilt Mansion (New York) Magnificent country home built in 1890's

Whitman Mission (Washington) Site where Indians killed missionaries Marcus Whitman and his wife

William Howard Taft (Ohio) President William H. Taft's birthplace

*Not yet open to the public. †Closed part of the year.

Canadian national parks

Auyuittuq* (Northwest Territories) Massive icecap and glaciers; fiords; only park above the Arctic Circle

Banff*† (Alberta) Rocky Mountain scenery with glaciers and hot springs; Banff and Lake Louise resort areas

Cape Breton Highlands*† (Nova Scotia) Rugged coastline and forested hills; seascapes from Cabot Trail

Elk Island* (Alberta) Rolling hills with aspen and spruce forests and many lakes; buffalo, deer, elk, and moose

Forillon* (Quebec) Scenic tip of Gaspé Peninsula that juts into Gulf of St. Lawrence

Fundy*† (New Brunswick) Rugged Bay of Fundy shoreline with coves and cliffs; some of world's highest tides

Georgian Bay Islands* (Ontario) Rock pillars, glacier-scraped rock, ancient Chippewa Indian ruins

Glacier*† (British Columbia) Alpine region in Selkirk Mountains with snowcapped peaks and over 100 glaciers

Gros Morne* (Newfoundland) Scenic Long Range Mountains, fiord-like lakes, waterfalls, beaches, and rugged seacoast

Jasper*† (Alberta) Rocky Mountain landscape with hot springs and lakes; Jasper resort area

Kejimkujik* (Nova Scotia) Rolling landscape with many islands and lakes; Indian rock etchings

Kluane* (Yukon Territory) Mount Logan in St. Elias Mountains; large glacier system; Dall sheep

Kootenay*† (British Columbia) Rocky Mountain scenery with broad valleys, glaciers, deep canyons, and hot springs

Kouchibouguac* (New Brunswick) Lagoons and bays; 15½-mile (24.9-kilometer) sweep of offshore sandbars

La Mauricie* (Quebec) Heavily wooded section of Laurentian Mountains with numerous lakes

Mount Revelstoke (British Columbia) Mountaintop plateau in Selkirk Mountains with alpine meadows and lakes

Nahanni* (Northwest Territories) Deep canyons; hot springs; Virginia Falls and Hell's Gate on South Nahanni River

Pacific Rim* (British Columbia) Long Beach and historic Life Saving Trail on west coast of Vancouver Island; sea lions

Point Pelee (Ontario) Bird migration flyways; Lake Frie beaches

Prince Albert*† (Saskatchewan) Interesting transition between northern forests and prairie grasslands; lakes and streams

Prince Edward Island*† (Prince Edward Island) Beaches, cliffs, dunes, and marshes; 25-mile (40-kilometer) strip on Gulf of St. Lawrence

Pukaskwa* (Ontario) Many lakes and rivers and wide variety of wildlife in wilderness area on Lake Superior

Riding Mountain*† (Manitoba) Forests, grasslands, and lakes on summit of Manitoba Escarpment

St. Lawrence Islands* (Ontario) Scenic islands and islets on St. Lawrence River

Terra Nova*† (Newfoundland) Spruce forest and bogs along rugged coastline; icebergs off shore in spring

Waterton Lakes*† (Alberta) Waterton-Glacier International Peace Park

Wood Buffalo* (Alberta-Northwest Territories border) Largest buffalo herd in North America and nesting grounds of rare whooping crane

Yoho*† (British Columbia) Rocky Mountain scenery with lakes, waterfalls, natural stone bridge, and Yoho Valley

*Camping permitted. †Has overnight lodging.

Canadian national historic parks and sites

Alexander Graham Bell (Nova Scotia) Museum with models of Bell's experiments

Artillery Park* (Quebec) French and British army buildings

Batoche* (Saskatchewan) Headquarters of métis during Saskatchewan Rebellion in 1885

Battle of the Chateauguay (Quebec) Site of War of 1812 battle

Battleford* (Saskatchewan) Fort of North-West Mounted Police during Saskatchewan Rebellion in 1885

Bellevue House (Ontario) Home of first prime minister of Canada, Sir John A. Macdonald, 1848 and 1849

Cape Spear* (Newfoundland) Lighthouse on Canada's most easterly point

Carleton Martello Tower* (New Brunswick) Defense post built during War of 1812

Cartier-Brébeuf Park (Quebec) Winter camp of Jacques Cartier in 1535-1536

Castle Hill* (Newfoundland) French and British fortifications of 1700's

Coteau-du-Lac* (Quebec) Site of British military post; historic canal

Fort Amherst* (Prince Edward Island) Ruins of a British fort built in 1758

Fort Anne* (Nova Scotia) Site of early Acadian settlement

Fort Beauséjour* (New Brunswick) Site of French fort built in 1750's; museum

Fort Chambly (Quebec) Site of French fort of early 1700's; museum

Fort Edward (Nova Scotia) Oldest blockhouse in Canada, built in 1750

Fort Espérance (Saskatchewan) Important North West Company post

Fort George* (Ontario) Reconstructed British fort from War of 1812

Fort Langley (British Columbia) Reconstruction of Hudson's Bay Company post

Fort Lennox* (Quebec) Site of British fort built during the early 1800's

Fort Lévis No. 1 (Quebec) Fortifications built by British, begun in 1865

Fort Malden (Ontario) Defense post built between 1797 and 1799

Fort Prince of Wales* (Manitoba) Fort built by Hudson's Bay Company, 1732-1772

Fort Rodd Hill (British Columbia) First lighthouse on Canada's west coast; fortifications built in late 1800's

Fort St. James* (British Columbia) Hudson's Bay Company post built in 1806

Fort St. Joseph* (Ontario) Trading post built in 1796; most westerly British fort

Fort Témiscamingue* (Quebec) Last of a series of posts built by fur traders

Fort Walsh* (Saskatchewan) Early post of North-West Mounted Police

Fort Wellington* (Ontario) British fort of the late 1830's

Fortress of Louisbourg* (Nova Scotia) Reconstruction of last French fort in Canada

Grand Pré* (Nova Scotia) Acadian village; home of Evangeline, heroine of Henry Wadsworth Longfellow's poem

Halifax Citadel (Nova Scotia) Restored British stone fort built in 1800's

Jacques Cartier Cross (Quebec) Commemorates Cartier's landing

Klondike Gold Rush International Historic Park* (Yukon Territory) Commemorates Klondike Gold Rush of 1897 and 1898; sites at Bonanza Creek, Dawson, Lake Bennett, and Whitehorse; Chilkoot and White Pass Trails; S. S. *Keno*, S. S. *Klondike*

L'Anse aux Meadows (Newfoundland) Authenticated Viking remains

Les Forges du Saint-Maurice* (Quebec) Site of Canada's first iron industry, 1729-1883

Lower Fort Garry* (Manitoba) Hudson's Bay Company fort built in 1830's

Maison Sir Wilfrid Laurier* (Quebec) Early home of Sir Wilfrid Laurier, Canada's seventh prime minister

National Battlefields Park (Quebec) Site of 1759 Battle of Plains of Abraham

Port au Choix (Newfoundland) Maritime Archaic Indians Burial site (2000? B.C.)

Port Royal Habitation* (Nova Scotia) Reconstruction of Habitation, a French fur-trading settlement of the early 1600's

Prince of Wales Martello Tower* (Nova Scotia) Restored defense fortification of early 1880's

Province House (Prince Edward Island) Birthplace of Confederation in 1864

Quebec City Walls and Gate (Quebec) Defense fortifications built by British in 1820's

Queenston Heights and Brock's Monument* (Ontario) Site of major British victory in War of 1812; monument honors General Isaac Brock

Rideau Canal (Ontario) Alternate shipping route to Upper Canada, built after War of 1812

Rocky Mountain House* (Alberta) Site of rival North West Company and Hudson's Bay Company trading posts

St. Andrews Blockhouse* (New Brunswick) Fortifications built at start of War of 1812

St. Roch (British Columbia) First ship to sail through the Northwest Passage from both the west and the east

Signal Hill (Newfoundland) Site of last battle of French and Indian War (1754-1763); reception of first transatlantic wireless telegraph message in 1901

Woodside (Ontario) Boyhood home of William Lyon Mackenzie King, prime minister of Canada for 21 years

York Factory* (Manitoba) Hudson's Bay Company fur-trading post, 1682-1957

York Redoubt* (Nova Scotia) Defense post dating from 1793

Source: Parks Canada. *Closed part of the year

Index of tourist sites

UNITED STATES

Travel information services

Alabama Bureau of Publicity & Information
532 South Perry Street
Montgomery, Alabama 36104

Alaska State Division of Tourism
Pouch E
Juneau, Alaska 99811

Arizona State Office of Tourism
3507 N. Central Avenue
Phoenix, Arizona 85012

Arkansas Division of Tourism
Department of Parks & Tourism
1 Capitol Mall
Little Rock, Arkansas 72201

California Office of Visitor Services
Department of Economic and Business Development
1030 13th Street, Suite 200
Sacramento, California 95814

Denver and Colorado Convention and Visitor's Bureau
225 W. Colfax Avenue
Denver, Colorado 80203

Connecticut Department of Economic Development
Tourism Division
210 Washington Street
Hartford, Connecticut 06106

Delaware State Travel Service
630 State College Road
P.O. Box 1401
Dover, Delaware 19901

Florida Division of Tourism
Collins Building
Tallahassee, Florida 32301

Georgia Tourist Division
Department of Industry and Trade
P.O. Box 1776
Atlanta, Georgia 30301

Hawaii Visitors Bureau
2270 Kalakaua Avenue, Suite 801
Honolulu, Hawaii 96815

Idaho Division of Economic & Community Affairs
State Capitol Building
Boise, Idaho 83720

Illinois Office of Tourism
310 South Michigan Avenue
10th Floor
Chicago, Illinois 60604

Indiana Tourism Development Division
Department of Commerce
400 North Meridian Street
Indianapolis, Indiana 46204

Iowa Development Commission Travel Division
250 Jewett Building
Des Moines, Iowa 50309

Kansas Department of Economic Development
Division of Travel & Tourism
503 Kansas Avenue, 6th Floor
Topeka, Kansas 66603

Kentucky Department of Tourism
Capital Plaza Tower, 22nd Floor
Frankfort, Kentucky 40601

Louisiana Office of Tourism
P.O. Box 44291, Capitol Station
Baton Rouge, Louisiana 70804

Maine Publicity Bureau
97 Winthrop Street
Hallowell, Maine 04347

Maryland Office of Tourism Development
Department of Economic and Community Development
1748 Forest Drive
Annapolis, Maryland 21401

Massachusetts Bureau of Tourism
100 Cambridge Street
Boston, Massachusetts 02202

Michigan Department of Commerce
Travel Bureau
P.O. Box 30226
Lansing, Michigan 48909

Minnesota Tourism Bureau
480 Cedar Street
St. Paul, Minnesota 55101

Mississippi Division of Tourism
Department of Economic Development
P.O. Box 849
Jackson, Mississippi 39205

Missouri Division of Tourism
Box 270
Jefferson City, Missouri 65102

Montana Travel Promotion Unit
Department of Commerce
Helena, Montana 59620

Nebraska Department of Economic Development
Travel & Tourism Division
P.O. Box 94666
Lincoln, Nebraska 68509

Nevada Department of Economic Development
Division of Tourism
Capitol Complex
1050 East Williams
Carson City, Nevada 89710

New Hampshire Vacation Center
P.O. Box 856
Concord, New Hampshire 03301

New Jersey Division of Travel & Tourism
CN-384
Trenton, New Jersey 08625

New Mexico Tourism & Travel Division
Commerce & Industry Department
Bataan Memorial Building
Santa Fe, New Mexico 87503

New York State Division of Tourism
Department of Commerce
99 Washington Avenue
Albany, New York 12245

North Carolina Division of Travel & Tourism
430 North Salisbury Street
Raleigh, North Carolina 27611

North Dakota State Travel Division
Capitol Grounds
Bismarck, North Dakota 58505

Ohio Office of Travel & Tourism
Department of Economic & Community Development
P.O. Box 1001
Columbus, Ohio 43216

Oklahoma Tourism & Recreation Department
Division of Tourism Promotion
505 Will Rogers Building
Oklahoma City, Oklahoma 73105

Oregon Department of Transportation
Travel Information Section
101 Transportation Building
Salem, Oregon 97310

Pennsylvania Bureau of Travel Development
Department of Commerce
416 Forum Building
Harrisburg, Pennsylvania 17120

Rhode Island Department of
Economic Development
Tourist Promotion Division
7 Jackson Walkway
Providence, Rhode Island 02903

South Carolina Department of
Parks, Recreation & Tourism
Suite 113
1205 Pendleton Street
Columbia, South Carolina 29201

South Dakota Division of Tourism
Pierre, South Dakota 57501

Tennessee Department of Tourist
Development
P.O. Box 23170
Nashville, Tennessee 37202

TEXAS
Department MG
Highway Department
Box 5064
Austin, Texas 78763

Utah Travel Council
Council Hall - Capitol Hill
Salt Lake City, Utah 84114

Vermont Travel Division
61 Elm Street
Montpelier, Vermont 05602

Virginia State Travel Service
202 North Ninth Street
Richmond, Virginia 23219

Washington Travel Development
Division
Department of Commerce &
Economic Development
General Administration Building
Olympia, Washington 98504

West Virginia Travel Development
Division
Office of Economic & Community
Development
State Capitol
Charleston, West Virginia 25305

Wisconsin Division of Tourism
Box 7606
Madison, Wisconsin 53707

Wyoming Travel Commission
I-25 at College Drive
Cheyenne, Wyoming 82002

For information regarding travel in Canada, contact:
Tourism Canada
235 Queen Street, 4th Floor East
Ottawa, Ontario K1A0H6
Canada

World Book Encyclopedia, Inc., offers a selection of fine porcelain collectible products including *For A Mother's Love Figurine* series. For subscription information write WORLD BOOK ENCYCLOPEDIA, INC., P.O. Box 3405, Chicago, IL 60654.